Back in the Days of Jesus: Gospel Homilies for Children

Luke

Living the Good News, Inc.
a division of The Morehouse Publishing Group
Editorial Offices
600 Grant Street, Suite 400
Denver, CO 80203

James R. Creasey, Publisher

Homilies by Dina Gluckstern and Dirk deVries

Editorial Staff: Joanne Youngquist, Kathleen Mulhern, Dirk deVries, Liz Riggleman,
  Dina Gluckstern, Kathy Coffey
Prepress/Production Staff: Sue MacStravic, Noel Taylor, Val Price, Meg Sandoval Phillips
Cover Design and Layout: Val Price, Sue MacStravic
Illustrations: Marcy Ramsey, Anne Kosel, Ansgar Holmberg, Betsy Johnson, Victoria Bergesen

Printed in the United States of America.

The scripture quotations used herein are from the Today's English Version, ©1992, American Bible Society. Used by permission.

ISBN 1-889108-00-6 (Volume 3)
ISBN 1-889108-04-9 (4 Volume Set)

Table of Contents

Introduction

You invite them forward with a mixture of both joy and apprehension, these children of assorted sizes and ages. Adults shift to allow the escape from cramped pews and closely packed chairs. Small forms drop out into the aisles, then bob forward toward the front of the church, some holding hands, some looking back questioningly at parents. Many grin; others share your apprehension. They surround you, watching you closely, waiting for your smile, your touch, your greeting. You know you take a risk each time you welcome this unpredictable group forward, but you also know, as you settle together at the front of the church, that the next few minutes will be among the most rewarding of your week.

Each parish calls it something different: a children's message, perhaps, or a children's sermon or children's talk. Here we refer to it as a children's homily, a short presentation, based on the day's gospel reading, that invites the children to enter into and experience the story of our faith. Each homily respects the children's own spiritual vitality, urging them to share their experience of God, themselves and each other in an environment of love and safety.

Why offer children their own homily?

Offering a children's homily says to the children: "This is a special time just for you, because *church is for you, too.* Here, in church, you are welcomed, delighted in, treasured, held in our arms as you are held in God's arms." A children's homily extends in a concrete way the embrace of our loving God to include these, God's most vulnerable children. "You are this important to us," is the message, as the children file forward to gather for their homily.

But a children's homily offers the children more than the important affirmation that church is their place, too. A well-prepared children's homily couches the basics of Christian experience in terms the children understand and own. It invites children to experience the truths of scripture from the inside out: Children don't learn *about* Jesus calming the storm, they imagine themselves, frightened and rain-soaked, clinging to the sides of the rocking boat, yearning for safety, holding their breath for the moment when Jesus says "Peace, be still," feeling the relief that Jesus brings to the storms they experience in day-to-day life.

Children don't learn about the comfort of Jesus' hug, they exchange Jesus' hugs with each other, then take those hugs out into the congregation. You get the idea.

And the benefits of a children's homily go farther than the children themselves. If you regularly present children's homilies, you already know how often adults approach you after the service and say, "That was great. I got more out of your children's homily than the regular homily." A children's homily—perhaps *because* it presents its point so simply and clearly, with the added framework of childlike wonder and innocence—can profoundly impress and move. Never underestimate the power of a child's fresh perspective or sudden and unexpected insight.

Many of the adults watching from the pews don't have children, or have little regular contact with small children. The children's homily helps balance their lives with the wonder and delight the children take in these encounters with God and scripture.

In addition, when you present the children's homilies, you model for families, friends and relatives ways to engage the children they love in the journey of faith. Storytelling, movement, songs, games and the use of props and illustrations—all of these explore faith in simple ways that others can use as well. After a month or two of watching children's homilies, people begin to catch on, even unconsciously adopting the methods demonstrated in your children's homilies.

Who are these homilies for?

Back in the Days of Jesus: Gospel Homilies for Children from the Gospel of Luke contains forty-six homilies, written for children from the age of four or five through eleven or twelve. Admittedly, this is a broad age range, and you may find some homilies seem more appropriate for the younger children than the older. We have attempted to provide something for all ages in each homily, including occasionally offering options within the homilies themselves. Keep in mind that a children's homily is not an instructional activity, and that age matters less when sharing in ritual and worship. In fact, a variety of responses can enrich the experience for all participants. You may want to invite older children to help younger children with certain tasks and responses. The older children will benefit from the sense of awe and wonder—the raw spirituality—of the younger children.

These homilies will work for both small and large groups, from less than half a dozen to as many as thirty or more. When appropriate, we suggest ways to change the homily for very small or very large groups; for example, in a large group, you may not be able to invite every child to offer a response to every question; do your best to let different children answer each question. In a small group, you may be able to reproduce a simple prop for each child to take home. For the most part, the size of the group will not matter, but if it does, you should be able to adapt each homily for the number of children you anticipate coming forward.

If you regularly have a larger group (more than twelve), consider recruiting another adult or teenage helper for each additional six or so children. This is particularly helpful when the homily includes more complex activities, or if another leader can provide a calming influence for restless children.

How do I prepare?

Each homily in this book includes:
- a scripture reference
- a quote from the reading
- a brief summary of both the reading and the homily
- a materials list
- directions for the homily
- a suggestion for closing prayer

We encourage you to begin your preparation by reading the scripture on which the homily is based. You might consider reading the story in two Bible versions, including *Today's English Version,* used in the preparation of these homilies. Think about the passage. You might ask yourself:
- What does this reading say to me?
- What truth about God, about others or about myself do I learn from this reading?

Then extend your question to include the children you anticipate will join you for the homily:
- What would I like the children to hear in this story?
- What does this reading say to them about the love and care of God?

After your own consideration of the reading, read through the summary of the reading and the homily, check the materials list and read once through the homily itself.

Most homilies in this book offer both an age-appropriate retelling of the gospel story and at least one activity to help the children enter into the meaning of the story (occasionally both story and activity are blended into one overall activity). Time limitations or personal preference may require that you use one or the other rather than both. Feel free to do so. The stories can stand alone; if you wish, a question or two taken from the activity may be enough to help you draw a story-only homily to a conclusion. Likewise, you may not wish to retell the gospel story if it has just been read from the Bible or lectionary; in this case, simply follow the regular reading of scripture with the homily activity.

Once you decide how much of the homily you wish to present, gather your materials and practice telling the story. We encourage you to memorize the story, though you may certainly use your own words if you wish. Tell the story to yourself, a friend or a family member once or twice. Inexperienced at storytelling? Familiarize yourself with the two cardinal rules of storytelling—make eye contact with your listeners and make sure they can hear you!

At the conclusion of each homily we offer a prayer. Again, add to or adapt each prayer as you wish.

Some basic principles to keep in mind:
- *The younger the children, the shorter the homily.* One guide-

line suggests that children will sit still and listen one minute for each year of their age; for example, the average five-year-old will be there, attending to you, for five minutes, an eight-year-old for eight minutes. Keep that in mind at points in the homily when you are doing the talking, for example, during a non-participatory story. That's why these homilies incorporate lots of feedback and interaction.

■ *There are more people involved than you and the children.* The parishioners listen and participate along with the children. Face the parishioners as you sit down to present the homily. Speak loudly, slowly and clearly. Repeat answers given by children if the children speak too softly for the parishioners to hear. If you use a poster or another prop, make it big enough —and hold it up high enough— for the parishioners to see, too. If children participate in actions (other than in a circle or semi-circle facing inward), face them toward the parishioners. While you and the children are not performing for the parishioners, you do invite them to worship with you. Keep that in mind.

■ *Respect what children say.* You don't need to correct the children, you need only allow them to experience the story for themselves, to find their own meaning and, if they wish, to articulate that meaning. God reveals God's self to children, as to adults, in the right ways at the right times. Trust God to do this in your children's homilies.

In the homily, affirm all children for their responses; a simple thank-you accomplishes this beautifully. You can also say, "Jared, you believe..." or "De-anna, you feel like...," reflecting back to children what they have shared. Acknowledge each child's right to believe and feel whatever he or she believes and feels without editorializing. At times you may be hoping the children suggest a specific idea; if they do not, simply suggest the idea yourself. Your ideas matter too, and the children want to hear them.

■ *Expect the unexpected.* In these homilies you invite open responses from creative, uninhibited children. You cannot control what they say or do (nor would you want to). If they perceive you as a caring friend, they will want to tell you about their pets, toys, eating habits and other topics that you may prefer not to discuss when you are leading in front of your parishioners. This will happen. Expect it, flow with it and enjoy it. Welcome even off-the-wall comments with grace and good humor, but be cautious not to laugh at the children, even when the parishioners do. A child can easily feel hurt if a serious comment shared in trust is met with laughter. Show your respect for the children by responding appreciatively to whatever they say.

Deal with the unexpected comment by acknowledging the child and redirecting attention back to the story or activity. If a child continues, you can thank him or her for the desire to share and explain that now you would like to focus on the activity or story at hand. Ask the child, "May I listen to your story later, after church?" Be sure to follow through with the child later. You might also put your finger to your lips and say, "This is our quiet time, our time to listen to the story. Can you do that for us?"

It always helps to remember: The clearest message to the children does not come through the content of your homily, but through the loving relationship you offer them when you gather together.

On Sunday morning, make sure to bring your collected materials and this book. Take a few minutes for a final review. Place any needed materials unobtrusively near the area where you will gather the children.

We recommend that you gather at the front of the church. Children can sit in a semicircle around you on the floor. If the floor is not car-peted, consider purchasing a large square carpet remnant to make sitting more comfortable. Many churches have several low steps at the front of the church; you could sit on one of these or on a low stool. You could, of course, also sit with the children on the floor.

Once you and the children settle in, begin the homily. Look with love and respect at each young face before you. You are in for a treat; these children have invited you into a most sacred circle. Consider yourself honored...and see what God will do.

Dirk deVries

One final note: Looking for a reading not covered in this volume? That reading may have a parallel in one or more of the other gospels—Matthew, Mark or John. Look in the other volumes in *Back in the Days of Jesus: Gospel Homilies for Children* and you may find the homily you seek.

Luke 1:26-38

"I am the Lord's servant," said Mary; "may it happen to me as you have said." And the angel left her. (Luke 1:38, _Today's English Version_)

Summary

In this reading from the Gospel of Luke, the angel announces to Mary that she will bear the Son of God. In today's homily, children first share good news of their own, then hear the good news in today's story.

Materials

Bible

Homily

Invite the children to come forward for today's homily. Ask them to sit in a semicircle around you.

Begin the homily by explaining to the children that they will share some good news with one another. Begin by _briefly_ telling some good news of your own.

Invite children to take turns sharing good things that are happening in their lives. Remember: Do not insist that every child volunteer, since some children may not feel happy this particular morning.

When all those who wish to share have done so, explain that in today's story there is good news, too.

Hold the Bible open to the Gospel of Luke as you tell today's story:

Mary was walking along a dusty road in Galilee, heading to the well. She and her mother had spent the morning cleaning, baking and talking. They were busy planning Mary's wedding, which was coming soon.

Bugs buzzed in the hot air. The heat made Mary feel dreamy. When she came to the well, she sat on its ledge and stared into the deep water below.

At that moment, the angel Gabriel, a messenger from God, appeared to Mary. He startled her, saying, "_Shalom_. Peace be with you, Mary. God is with you and God blesses you greatly."

Mary was deeply troubled by these strange words. What could they mean? But the angel went on, "Do not be afraid. You will become pregnant, today, with a son. He will become king of a kingdom that will never end."

Mary asked, "How can that be? I'm not even married yet!"

Gabriel explained, "God's power will make you pregnant.

Your cousin, Elizabeth, is pregnant, too, and people thought she was too old to ever have a baby."

"How can this be?" asked Mary.

"God's power can do anything," said Gabriel.

Mary still did not understand all that the angel said, but she did know one thing. She loved God, with all her heart. "I am God's own," she answered. "Let everything that you have said happen to me."

Then Mary was alone. She filled her jug. She turned for home. She lifted her eyes to the sky and whispered, "I am God's own."

If you wish, discuss with the children:
- What good news did we hear in today's story?
- Who do you think Mary's baby would be? *(As necessary, clarify that the expected baby is Jesus.)*

Prayer

- Dear God, thanks for sending good news to Mary. And thanks for Jesus; he's the *best* good news of all! *Amen.*

Thank the children for joining you and invite them to return to their seats.

Luke 1:39-45

Mary said, "My heart praises the Lord; my soul is glad because of God my Savior, for he has remembered me, his lowly servant!" (Luke 1:46-48a, *Today's English Version*)

Summary

In this reading from the Gospel of Luke, Mary visits Elizabeth and shares with her the joy of her holy pregnancy. In today's homily, children participate in the telling of the story, then join Mary in thanking God for the baby Jesus.

Materials

Bible
two poster-board signs, one reading *Mary's House* and one reading *Elizabeth's House*
tape or tacks
blankets or floor pillows

Before the homily post the two signs on opposite sides of the church, toward the front of the church. Spread a blanket or several floor pillows on the floor in front of each sign to mark each "house."

Homily

Invite the children to come forward for today's homily. Ask them to sit together in "Mary's house."

Invite the children to clap a steady rhythm as they learn this chant:

Walking, **walk**ing,
Over the **hills** to
Eliz**a**beth's **house**.

Clap on the bold-faced syllables. Repeat the chant until children know it. Explain:
- Christmas is Jesus' birthday. In the weeks before Christmas, we get ready for Jesus' birthday.
- The first person who got ready for Jesus' birthday was his mother, Mary, and that's the story I want to tell you today.
- The chant we've learned will help us tell today's story.

Hold the Bible open to the Gospel of Luke as you tell today's story:

Mary was a young woman who lived long ago. One day God sent an angel to Mary.

The angel said, "Your cousin Elizabeth is going to have a baby. And you will have a baby too. You will be the mother of baby Jesus, God's own Son!"

Mary said, "Yes! I will do what God wants."

Then the angel left.

"I can hardly wait," said Mary. "I want to see Elizabeth, and tell her the good news."

(At this point in the story, lead the children in a march from "Mary's house" to "Elizabeth's house." Help the children clap and chant as they move. At "Elizabeth's house," seat the children and continue:)

"Look!" said Elizabeth. "I see Mary! She's coming to visit me."

Elizabeth ran to meet Mary. "I am so happy to see you. We are both going to have babies!" She hugged Mary.

Mary said, "How did you know I was going to have a baby?"

Elizabeth said, "Because my own baby is jumping for joy inside me."

The two women hugged. They danced. They sang.

Mary sang a special song. "I praise my God, for God has done great things for me."

Mary stayed with Elizabeth for many days, and Mary and Elizabeth were happy together.

After the story, say:
- We still remember Mary's song today.
- The whole song is too long for us to learn today, but we can use part of it to say thank you to God.

Show children how to accompany this chant, again with a steady clapping rhythm. The bold-faced syllables are said on the claps:

I **praise** my **God**,
for **God** has **done**
great **things** for **me**.

With the children, repeat the chant several times. Ask:
- For what special things can we thank God?

Accept all answers. If necessary, add this one:
- We can thank God for baby Jesus, too.
- Let's chant Mary's song to thank God for baby Jesus.

Prayer

Repeat the chant once or twice more, this time inviting the parishioners to join in.

Thank the children for joining you and invite them to return to their seats.

Luke 2:1-21

She gave birth to her son, wrapped him in clothes and laid him in a manger—there was no room for them in stay in the inn. (Luke 2:7, *Today's English Version*)

Summary

In this reading from the Gospel of Luke, Mary gives birth to Jesus, and shepherds and angels celebrate his birth. In today's homily, children hear this familiar story, then reflect on their families as they prepare a bed for the baby Jesus.

Materials

Bible
manger, cradle or basket
straw
infant doll
baby blanket

Homily

Invite the children to come forward for today's homily. Ask them to sit in a semicircle around you.

Begin the homily by teaching children to recite this story chant:
■ Good News! Jesus is born!

Where indicated in the story, invite the children to say this chant together.

Hold the Bible open to the Gospel of Luke as you tell today's story:

"Go to your home towns," ordered the rulers. "We want to count the people."

So Mary and Joseph made the long, hard trip to Bethlehem. The little town was very crowded. All the houses and inns were full. Mary and Joseph had to stay in a small barn!

While they were there, Mary's time came. *(Chant.)* Mary gave birth to a son, Jesus. *(Chant.)*

She wrapped him in warm cloths and laid him in the manger—the animals' feeding dish, soft with hay. *(Chant.)*

Out in the country, shepherds took care of their sheep. Suddenly, an angel appeared to them! *(Chant.)* The shepherds were afraid, but the angel said, "Don't be afraid! I bring you good news. *(Chant.)*

"Today in Bethlehem, Jesus is born! Jesus is the One who will make you free. *(Chant.)*

"Go and see him! He is wrapped in cloths and lying in a manger!" *(Chant.)*

15

Suddenly, the sky was filled with bright angels! They sang, "Glory to God! Happy are God's people! Good news!"

"Let's go see this baby," said the shepherds. "Let's go see the good news." *(Chant.)*

The shepherds hurried to the barn to see Jesus. They found everything just as the angel had told them. *(Chant.)*

When the shepherds left, they told everyone they met: *(Chant.)*

Back in the barn, Mary sat and held her baby. She sang softly to Jesus and said: *(Chant.)*

Place the empty cradle or basket and a large pile of straw within the children's reach. Explain that each time they offer an answer to today's story questions, they may place a handful of straw in the cradle or basket to soften a bed for the baby Jesus.

Questions:
- In today's gospel story, what does Mary do for the baby Jesus?
- What do our mothers do for us? *(Encourage many answers.)*
- What do our fathers do for us? *(Encourage many answers.)*
- What do we do for each other? *(Encourage many answers.)*

Once the cradle or basket has been filled with straw, invite a child to place a baby blanket and the infant doll in the cradle or basket. Say:
- There, now we've made a warm, safe bed for the baby Jesus!

Prayer

Sing softly a verse of "Away in the Manger" as you and the children kneel around the completed cradle.

Thank the children for joining you and invite them to return to their seats.

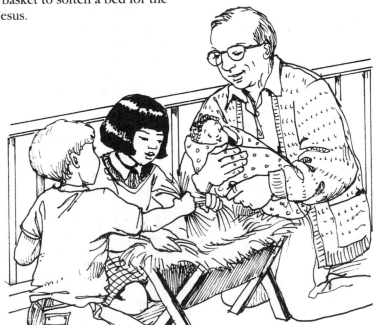

Luke 2:22-40

The time came for Joseph and Mary to perform the ceremony of purification, as the Law of Moses commanded. So they took the child to Jerusalem to present him to the Lord... (Luke 2:22, *Today's English Version***)**

Summary

In this reading from the Gospel of Luke, Joseph and Mary present Jesus in the temple, where he is hailed as God's Messiah by Simeon and Anna. In today's homily, children first hear this story, then are themselves "presented" to the parish as special children of God.

Materials

Bible

Homily

Invite the children to come forward for today's homily. Ask them to sit in a semicircle around you.

Hold the Bible open to the Gospel of Luke as you tell today's story:

In the land of Israel was the holy city Jerusalem. In the city of Jerusalem was the holy temple of God. In the temple of God were two holy people: Simeon and Anna.

Day and night Simeon and Anna prayed to God.

"God, save Israel! Send us your Messiah, your chosen one!" prayed Simeon.

"God, set us free! Send us the leader who will free Jerusalem," prayed Anna.

Many years they prayed. Many years they waited. Simeon and Anna grew old, but still they waited for God's chosen one.

Now it was the custom of people of Jesus' time to dedicate their children to God. Joseph and Mary said to each other, "Let's bring Jesus to the temple. We can present him to God, so he will do God's work." As soon as Joseph and Mary carried the tiny baby into the temple, Simeon took him into his arms.

"Here he is," Simeon cried. "Now, God, I can die in peace, for you have shown me your chosen one, the one who will save Israel. He is the light of the world."

Anna came hurrying up. She touched the baby with gentle

fingers and called aloud, "Thank you, God! He is born at last!" And she called to the people around her. "Here is the one! Here is the child who will set us free!"

Mary and Joseph listened in wonder. When their prayers in the temple were finished, they took Jesus home and watched him grow. And he grew strong and full of wisdom. God was with him, indeed.

With the children, discuss:
- Why do Mary and Joseph take Jesus to the temple?
- What do Simeon and Anna say about Jesus when they see him at the temple?

Invite the children to stand side by side in a single row, facing the parishioners. Say:
- And now I present to the church, these special children of God as well. They are here to do God's work, just like Jesus.

- Here is *(name the first child)*, she (he) is chosen by God.
- This is *(name the next child)*, he (she) is God's light for the world.
- I now present *(name the next child)*, she (he) has much to teach us.

Continue for the remaining children, presenting each with a brief statement of that child's favored place in God's community. Other affirming statements you might make include:
- ...is growing in strength and wisdom, just like Jesus.
- ...has God with her (him), every day.
- ...is doing good things for God.
- ...shows the love of God to his (her) family and friends.

Prayer

- God, we are glad that Mary and Joseph dedicated Jesus to serving and loving you. Each of these children are here to love and serve you, too. *Amen.*

Luke 2:41-52

Jesus grew both in body and in wisdom, gaining favor with God and people. (Luke 2:52, *Today's English Version*)

Summary

In this reading from the Gospel of Luke, the boy Jesus stays behind at the temple in Jerusalem, talking with the teachers, while his parents head back to Nazareth. In today's homily, children first act out the story as it is told, then discuss ways in which they, like Jesus, grow in strength and wisdom.

Materials

Bible

Homily

Invite the children to come forward for today's homily. Ask them to *stand* in a semicircle around you.

As you tell today's story, invite children to act out what's happening, as indicated. Hold the Bible open to the Gospel of Luke as you tell the story:

Jesus—who was just twelve years old—his parents and their friends walked and walked and walked, all the way from Nazareth, where they lived, to Jerusalem, where they were to celebrate the Passover Festival. Let's pretend we're walking to Jerusalem...

The Passover Festival was a noisy, joyful event. There were people *everywhere*. Mary, Joseph and Jesus saw friends and relatives that they had not seen in a long time. They ate and danced and sang together. They thanked and praised God. Let's pretend we are at the Passover Festival, too, having a good time with our friends, remembering God's faithfulness...

The Passover Festival ended, and it was time to go home. Mary and Joseph and their friends packed their things and started walking, walking, walking back to Nazareth. Let's pretend we're walking home to Nazareth...

Suddenly, Mary asked Joseph, "Have you seen Jesus?"

"No," said Joseph. "But he must be around here somewhere; let's check with our other friends."

Joseph and Mary asked the friends they were traveling with, "Have you seen Jesus? Have you seen Jesus?" Everyone looked around for Jesus. Let's pretend we're looking around for Jesus...

Jesus was not to be found! "We've traveled all day without him," Mary frowned.

"You don't suppose he's still back in Jerusalem?" Joseph asked.

So Mary and Joseph turned around and went walking, walking, walking, all the way back to Jerusalem. Let's pretend we're walking back to Jerusalem...

Well, do you know where they found Jesus? In the temple, talking with the Jewish teachers. He was asking questions, but he was also *answering* questions! People were amazed at the answers given by this twelve-year-old boy! Let's pretend we've been listening to Jesus' answers. Let's pretend we're amazed too...

But Mary and Joseph were angry. "Son, why have you done this? We've been so worried about you! We were afraid something had happened to you!" Let's pretend we're Mary and Joseph. Let's pretend we're angry, too...

Jesus said to his parents, "Didn't you know this was where I'd be, in my Father's house?" Mary and Joseph didn't understand. They scratched their heads and wondered. Let's pretend to be Mary and Joseph, wondering...

But Jesus went back home with his parents, walking, walking, walking all the way back to Nazareth. He was obedient to them. And he grew stronger. And he grew wiser. And as he grew, he pleased God.

Thank the children for helping you tell the story and invite them to be seated. Discuss:

- Jesus was once a child, just like us. He grew and grew, just as we are growing and growing.
- Jesus grew up strong.
  — What do you think helped Jesus grow up strong?
  — What helps us to grow up strong?
- Jesus grew up wise, knowing right from wrong.
  — What do you think helped Jesus to grow up wise, knowing right from wrong?
  — What helps us to grow up knowing right from wrong?
- Jesus grew up pleasing God.
  — What do you think helped Jesus to grow up pleasing God?
  — What helps us to grow up pleasing God?

Prayer

- Dear Jesus, help us to grow up strong, wise and holy, just as you did. *Amen.*

Thank the children for joining you and invite them to return to their seats.

Luke 3:1-6

**As it is written in the book of Isaiah:
"Someone is shouting in the desert:
'Get the road ready for the Lord;
make a straight path for
him to travel!'" (Luke 3:4,**
Today's English Version)

Summary

In this reading from the Gospel of Luke, John the Baptist brings his message of repentance, baptism and preparation. In today's homily, children first hear this story, then silently consider how they would prepare for a visit from Jesus.

Materials

Bible

Homily

Invite the children to come forward for today's homily. Ask them to sit in a semicircle around you.

Begin the homily by teaching children this response:

Homilist: Who's coming?

Children: Jesus is coming.

To help children learn the response, encourage them to vary the response by whispering, singing, speaking high or low, etc. Explain to the children that they can help tell today's homily by calling out the answer whenever they hear the question.

Hold the Bible open to the Gospel of Luke as you tell today's story:

Who's coming?

Jesus is coming!

John the Baptist walks among the people. John says, "Jesus is coming!"

The people say, "Who's coming?"

Jesus is coming!

John the Baptist says, "Make a straight path for Jesus. Get a road ready for Jesus, because he's coming to be with all God's people."

The people say, "How do we make a straight path? How do we get a road ready?

"And who's coming?"

Jesus is coming!

John the Baptist says, "Turn away from your sins. Be baptized. Start a new life today. That's how you can get ready for the one who is coming."

Who's coming?

Jesus is coming!

"Yes," says John the Baptist. "So get ready!"

Invite children (and the parishioners) to close their eyes and to silently imagine:

■ Your mom or dad has just told you that Jesus is coming to your house tonight. How do you feel about this news? (*Pause.*)

■ What would you want to do to get ready for Jesus' visit? What would you want to do in your room? in your house? in your heart? (*Pause.*)

■ How long would you like Jesus to stay? just for dinner? overnight? for a week? forever? (*Pause.*)

■ What would you do to get ready for Jesus if he came to live with you? (*Pause.*)

Allow a minute for silent reflection, then invite the children to share what they pictured. Be sure to repeat quiet responses so that the parishioners can hear them.

Discuss:

■ Jesus really does live with us, in our hearts and minds. How can we make sure Jesus feels welcome there?

Prayer

■ Thank you Jesus, for being with us right now. We welcome you. *Amen.*

Thank the children for joining you and invite them to return to their seats.

Luke 3:7-18

In many different ways John preached the Good News to the people and urged them to change their ways. (Luke 3:18, *Today's English Version*)

Summary

In this reading from the Gospel of Luke, John the Baptist preaches justice and announces the coming of Jesus, the Messiah. In today's homily, children hear this story, then brainstorm and practice ways to follow God.

Materials

Bible
newsprint or poster board on which you have written *follow God* in large letters

Homily

Invite the children to come forward for today's homily. Ask them to sit in a semicircle around you.

Hold the Bible open to the Gospel of Luke as you tell today's story:

John the Baptist stood at the top of the hill. Around him sat his friends and followers, listening as he taught. "We all must turn from our sins and follow God!" he shouted. "God is ready to see who will follow God and who will not!"

The people asked, "What are we to do, John?" They wanted to follow God, but they weren't sure how.

"If you have clothes, share them with people who are cold. If you have food, share it with those who are hungry."

People who took money from others unfairly asked, "And John, what are *we* to do? How can *we* follow God?"

"Stop cheating others," John said.

Soldiers came to John and asked, "And what about *us*? What are *we* to do to follow God?"

John said to the soldiers: "Don't use your strength to cheat or hurt people. Be honest in your work."

The people liked what John said. They were glad to know what they could do to follow God. "Could John be the Messiah, God's special messenger?" they asked one another.

"No," said John, "but the Messiah is on his way. He is greater than I, and you are to follow him when you find him."

And so John taught people how to follow God, and how to get ready for the Messiah, Jesus.

Show the poster board or newsprint prepared **before the homily**. Ask:
- Who can read the two words on our poster (or newsprint) for us?
- That's right, *follow God*. In today's story, John the Baptist told the people to get ready for Jesus by following God:
  — How did John say the people could follow God?
  — What other ways do we know to follow God?

Encourage many responses to this final question; for example:
- We follow God when we feed the hungry, help the sick, comfort the lonely, etc.

- We follow God when we use kind words.

Continue:
- How could we follow God this morning, right now, right here in church?

Again, encourage many responses to this question, this time being alert to any suggestions from the children that you could implement immediately, before the concluding prayer. Children might suggest:
- praying
- singing
- giving each other a hug
- giving to the church
- saying "hello" to someone who's lonely
- saying "I'm sorry" to a brother or sister
- saying "thank you" to someone

Implement as many of the children's suggestions as possible.

Prayer
- Dear God, help us to follow you, every day. *Amen*.

Thank the children for joining you and invite them to return to their seats.

Luke 3:15-22

After all the people had been baptized, Jesus also was baptized. While he was praying, heaven was opened, and the Holy Spirit came down upon him in bodily form like a dove. (Luke 3:21-22a, *Today's English Version*)

Summary

In this reading from the Gospel of Luke, John baptizes Jesus and God identifies Jesus as "my own dear Son." In today's homily, children explore and discuss water, then hear today's story.

Materials

Bible
large basin or tub of water
towels

Homily

Invite the children to come forward for today's homily. Ask them to sit in a semicircle around you.

Begin today's homily by inviting each child to put his or her hands into the water. Encourage the children to talk about water, what it looks like, what it feels like and what they use water for every day. You could ask questions such as:
■ What can we do *with* water?
■ What can we do *in* water?

Let children dry off as you say:
■ Once, something very important happened to Jesus in the water

of a river, and that's the story I want to tell you today.

Hold the Bible open to the Gospel of Luke as you tell today's story:

People came from far and wide to listen to John as he preached by the Jordan river. "You will see God's salvation," John preached to the people. "Turn away from doing wrong and live a new life for God."

John baptized these people; he dipped the people into the water and prayed that they would live new and better lives.

One day John heard a person say, "Maybe he's the Messiah."

"Yes," said several others. "Maybe he's the one God has sent to save us all."

John walked quickly to the people. "No," he said. "I baptize you with water, but someone is coming who is so great that he will baptize you with the Holy Spirit."

"Baptize us with the Holy Spirit!" a woman exclaimed. "What do you mean?"

"When I baptize you, the water of this river washes over you," John said. "But when the Messiah comes, the Holy Spirit, God's own power, will wash over you. God will give you power to live truly new lives."

"But you are so holy, John!" said a man. "How can anyone else be the Messiah?"

"I am not even holy enough to untie the Messiah's sandals," said John.

"The Messiah is someone holier than John?" the people whispered to each other. "What will he be like, this Messiah?"

Then one day Jesus—the true Messiah—came to the river. After all the people were baptized, Jesus waded into the water and walked to John. "Will you baptize me?" Jesus asked.

So John dipped Jesus into the water of the river. As Jesus came up from the water, the Holy Spirit of God came down upon Jesus like a dove.

And as John and Jesus prayed together, they heard God say, "Jesus, you are my own dear Son. I am pleased with you."

If you wish, discuss with the children:
- What happened to Jesus in today's story?
- When are people baptized here in our church?
- How was Jesus' baptism different from the baptisms we see in church? How was Jesus' baptism the same?
- When we are baptized, God's Holy Spirit pours over us just like the water does.
- Why do you think God wants to give each of us the Holy Spirit?

Accept the children's answers and be willing to state your own belief, a belief you might ponder **before the homily**. You might say that God gives us the Holy Spirit so that we can know God's love for us and share that love with others.

Prayer

- God, thank you for giving Jesus your love and Holy Spirit when he was baptized. Thank you for giving us your love and Holy Spirit, too. *Amen*.

Thank the children for joining you and invite them to return to their seats.

Luke 4:1-13

Jesus returned from the Jordan full of the Holy Spirit and was led by the Spirit into the desert, where he was tempted by the Devil for forty days. (Luke 4:1-2a, *Today's English Version***)**

Summary

In this reading from the Gospel of Luke, the devil tempts Jesus in the desert. In today's homily, children discuss temptation, then participate in an interactive telling of the story.

Materials

Bible
plate of tempting snacks

Homily

Invite the children to come forward for today's homily. Ask them to sit in a semicircle around you.

Place the plate of snacks in the middle of the semicircle. Make some appreciative comments and invite similar comments from the children:
- Mmmm...those look good.
- Those are my favorite; how about you?

Ask the children:
- What is *temptation?*
- What does it mean to be *tempted?*
- Do you find these snacks tempt-

ing? I'll put the snacks away for a while so we don't feel tempted.
- Jesus once was tempted, too, and that's the story I want to tell you today.

Hold the Bible open to the Gospel of Luke as you tell today's story. Invite the children to stand in a circle with you so they can help tell the story, too:

Jesus walks in the desert. It's very hot here in the desert. Feel the sun beating down? Feel the sweat dripping off the ends of our noses? Feel how thirsty we are? Feel how hungry we are? *(Invite children to act out any and all of these, for example, shading their eyes from the sun, wiping sweat from their faces, rubbing their stomachs in hunger, etc.)*

Suddenly, the devil stands right here with Jesus.

The devil says to Jesus, "You're very hungry aren't you?"

Jesus nods. *(Invite the children to nod, too.)*

"You've gone a long time without food, haven't you?"

Jesus nods again. (Children nod too.)

"Why don't you just turn this rock into a fresh loaf of bread? You can do that, can't you?"

Jesus nods again...(children nod)...but then starts to shake his head no. (Children shake heads no.) Jesus says, "No, devil! God will give me the food I need. Stop tempting me!"

And the devil goes away. (Invite children to show relief.)

But the devil comes back.

The devil says to Jesus, "Look out there, Jesus. See all those countries all over the world?"

Jesus nods. (Invite the children to nod, too.)

"Wouldn't it be fun to control all those countries? to have all their money?"

Jesus nods again. (Children nod too.)

"If you worship me, Jesus, I'll give it all to you. Wouldn't that be grand?"

Jesus nods again...(children nod)...but then starts to shake his head no. (Children shake heads no.) Jesus says, "No, devil! If God wants me to have power or money, God will give them to me. Stop tempting me!"

And the devil goes away. (Invite children to show relief.)

But the devil comes back.

The devil says to Jesus, "Look down there, Jesus. See how far down it is to the ground?" (Look down and shudder, as if looking down from a great height.)

Jesus nods. (Invite the children to nod, too.)

"Haven't you ever wanted to fly? To soar through the air like a bird? Wouldn't that be fun?"

Jesus nods again. (Children nod too.)

"You could do it right now, Jesus. God's angels will catch you before you hit the ground...but what a thrill on the way down, eh?"

Jesus nods again...(children nod)...but then starts to shake his head no. (Children shake heads no.) Jesus says, "No, devil! If God wants me to fly, he'll teach me to fly. Stop tempting me!"

And the devil goes away...and doesn't come back. (Invite children to show relief.)

Prayer

◼ Jesus, we're glad you resisted the devil's temptations. Help us to resist temptation too. *Amen.*

Share the snacks with the children. Thank the children for joining you and invite them to return to their seats.

Luke 4:14-30

All the people in the synagogue had their eyes fixed on him, as he said to them, "This passage of scripture has come true today, as you heard it being read." (Luke 4:20b-21, *Today's English Version*)

Summary

In this reading from the Gospel of Luke, Jesus teaches to—and faces the rejection of—the people of his hometown. In today's homily, children discuss times when it is difficult to speak the truth, then hear today's story.

Materials

Bible
drawing of boy printed on page 31

Homily

Invite the children to come forward for today's homily. Ask them to sit in a semicircle around you.

Begin the homily by showing children the drawing of the boy who has pulled all the flowers from the garden. Ask:
- What do you think has happened?
- What do you think he will do?

Ask the children to share times when they have had to tell the truth, even when it was hard. What did they do? How did they feel? Be careful not to offer moral judg-ments on the children's stories, calling some characters "honest" or "good" and others "dishonest" or "bad." Instead, offer comments that show you are listening with attention and empathy. *Examples:*
- Maria, it must have been very hard to tell the truth when your sister was so angry with you.
- Tricia, you had a difficult choice to make that day.

End the discussion by saying:
- Now let's hear a story about a time when Jesus told the truth.

Hold the Bible open to the Gospel of Luke as you tell today's story:

Jesus traveled many places, but one day he returned home. He entered the synagogue where people learned about and worshiped God. It was time for prayer.

The man in charge of the synagogue asked Jesus to read a passage of scripture.

Jesus stood. The scripture was written on a scroll, and Jesus unrolled the scroll to read this passage:

The Spirit of God is upon me. God has chosen me to tell good news. The time has come when God will save all God's people.

Jesus looked around the synagogue of his hometown. "I am the one God has chosen," he said again. "God has chosen me to save God's people."

The synagogue was silent. The people stared at Jesus, who had grown up in this same town. "Wasn't his father Joseph?" one of the people whispered.

"If he's the one God has chosen, why hasn't he worked any miracles here?" muttered another person.

Jesus knew what the people were thinking. "I tell you," he said, "I think people everywhere will welcome me more than you. You think you know all about me because I grew up here. You want to see for yourselves the miracles I have done elsewhere. But my work will be done as God wants, not as you want."

The eyes of the people grew hard. "How dare you speak to us like that!" they said. "How dare you!"

But Jesus didn't stop. He knew God wanted the people to hear the truth. "Listen to me," Jesus said. "Once there was no rain in Israel for three and a half years and food did not grow. People in Israel were hungry.

But God sent a man named Elijah, not to anyone in Israel, but only to a widow who lived far away."

The people grew angrier. But Jesus still didn't stop. "Many people in Israel suffered from a dreaded skin disease, too. But God sent a man named Elisha, not to anyone in Israel, but only to heal a man who lived far away."

"Don't let him speak to us like that!" yelled a voice in the synagogue. "God loves us, not foreigners!" The other people roared with anger. The crowd rose up and dragged Jesus out of town. The crowd was so rough that it almost pushed Jesus off a cliff.

But Jesus stopped the people without even touching them. I don't know how Jesus did this, but he simply walked away, right through the middle of the angry crowd. Then Jesus left his hometown, where no one would listen, and went on his way to do God's work.

Prayer

■ Dear God, help us to tell the truth as Jesus did, even when it is hard. *Amen.*

Thank the children for joining you and invite them to return to their seats.

For use with Luke 4:14-30, pp. 29-30.

OUR KING

Music traditional

1. Our King wears a crown and he car-ries a cross.
2. Our King brings new life for the whole world to know.
3. Our King rules for - ev - er. He lives in our hearts.

1. Our King wears a crown and he car-ries a cross.
2. Our King brings new life for the whole world to know.
3. Our King lives for - ev - er. He lives in our hearts.

1. Our King wears a crown and he car-ries a cross and his
2. Our King brings new life for the whole world to know and his
3. Our King rules for - ev - er. He lives in our hearts and his

1. name is Je - sus, our King!
2. name is Je - sus, our King!
3. name is Je - sus, our King!

For use with Luke 23:35-43, pp. 99-100.

Luke 5:1-11

Jesus said to Simon, "Don't be afraid; from now on you will be catching people" (Luke 5:10b, *Today's English Version*)

Summary

In this reading from the Gospel of Luke, Jesus' advice to Simon Peter yields an enormous catch of fish …and Jesus' first disciples. In today's homily, children first "fish" for each other, then hear today's story.

Materials

Bibles
fish shapes cut from colored construction paper
scissors
felt pens
paper clips
dowel or stick
string
small magnet
dishpan, bucket or blue cloth

Before the homily cut from construction paper one fish shape for each child. Attach a metal paper clip to the mouth end of each fish. Tie the magnet on a length of string to one end of the dowel or stick to make a fishing pole.

Homily

Invite the children to come forward for today's homily. Stand together to one side of the usual storytelling area.

Distribute one construction-paper fish shape to each child. Make available the felt markers.

Help children to write their names on their fish.

Put the fish shapes in a dishpan or bucket, or lay them on the blue cloth. Invite the children to "catch" other children for today's story. Each child uses the magnetic fishing pole to catch one fish.

Ask each child to bring the child he or she caught to the storytelling area. (Note that children who get "caught" before they "fish" will need to return to the "fish pond" even after they've been taken to the storytelling area.) When all the children are in the storytelling area, invite them to sit in a semicircle around you. Say:
■ We caught fish *and* people—just like the fishermen in today's story.

Hold the Bible open to the Gospel of Luke as you tell today's story:

Wherever Jesus went, crowds of people followed. One day, there were so many people, and they followed so closely, that Jesus thought they were going to push him right into the water behind him.

Jesus looked around. Simon, James and John sat in two boats. The three men were tired from a long night of fishing.

Jesus called to Simon. "Let me come into your boat. The people will be able to see me and hear me—and I won't land in the sea!"

Simon laughed and made room for Jesus. He listened to Jesus teach. He liked what Jesus had to say.

When Jesus was finished, he turned to Simon with a smile. "Thank you! Now let me do something for you. Row out to the deep water and let down your fish net."

Simon groaned. "Lord, I've been fishing all night. There's just no fish around for me to catch. But if you say so, I'll give it a try."

Simon rowed into the deep water and let down his net over the side. And the net filled with fish—so many fish that Simon thought his nets would break!

"James! John!" he yelled. "Help me!"

James and John rowed their boat quickly to Simon. They cast their own nets over the side, and the three fishers pulled and tugged until they had hauled in enough fish to fill both boats.

They were amazed. Simon looked at Jesus and his eyes filled with tears. "Oh, Jesus," he said, "you shouldn't be in this boat with me. I can tell that you come from God, and I'm just a sinner. I'm not good enough to be your friend."

But Jesus smiled and put his arm around Peter's shoulder. "Simon, you *are* my friend. Don't worry—just come with me. And you won't catch only fish: you'll catch men and women and girls and boys for God."

And Simon, James and John left their boats. They left their fish. They left everything and followed Jesus to catch many people for God.

If you wish, discuss with the children:
- What do you think it means to catch people for God?
- How might *we* catch people for God?

Prayer
- Thank you, Jesus, for inviting Simon, James, John *and all of us* to catch people for God. *Amen*.

Thank the children for joining you and invite them to return to their seats.

Luke 6:27-38

"Love your enemies and do good to them; lend and expect nothing back. You will then have a great reward... Be merciful just as your Father is merciful." (Luke 6:35a, 36, *Today's English Version*)

Summary

In this reading from the Gospel of Luke, Jesus calls his followers to reflect God's mercy and generosity —even to their enemies. In today's homily, children first sing a song about God's generosity, then hear today's story.

Materials

Bible
scoop
bowl of dry rice, lentils or other small items that can be easily scooped

Homily

Invite the children to come forward for today's homily. Ask them to sit in a semicircle around you.

Teach the children these words to the tune of "He's Got the Whole World in His Hands":

> We've got the whole world from God's hands.
> We've got the whole world from God's hands.
> We've got the whole world from God's hands.
> We've got the whole world from God's hands.

Encourage children to make up new verses for the song by thinking of gifts God gives us. *Examples*:
- We've got mothers and fathers from God's hands...
- We've got pepperoni pizza from God's hands...

Children may also want to clap in time to the singing. If it feels appropriate, invite the parishioners to join in, too.

At the end of the song, say:
- God gives us so many gifts. Let's listen to what Jesus says about giving.

Use the scoop as a focal point for today's story. When you reach the point marked *pour*, pour a scoop of rice into your hand—over the bowl—until your hand is filled and overflowing. Hold the Bible open to the Gospel of Luke as you tell today's story:

Jesus walked down from a hill. He saw his many friends wait-

ing for him: Joanna, Peter, Mary Magdalene, James. They were ready to listen to Jesus.

And Jesus said, "Give to others and God will give to you.

"Give a blessing; pray for others. Give clothing; keep others warm. Give others what you want to have yourself.

"Don't just give to people you like! Don't just give to nice, friendly people!

"But give to people you don't like, even your enemies. That's how God gives—to all kinds of people.

"Give freely to others, and God will give freely to you (*pour*), pouring out good things for you until they overflow.

"What you give to others, God will give to you."

Prayer

■ Jesus, help us to give as God gives, overflowing with kindness to everyone. *Amen.*

Thank the children for joining you and invite them to return to their seats.

Luke 6:43-45

"A healthy tree does not bear bad fruit, nor does a poor tree bear good fruit. Every tree is known by the fruit it bears..." (Luke 6:43-44a, *Today's English Version*)

Summary

In this reading from the Gospel of Luke, Jesus teaches that our words and behavior reveal our relationship to God. In today's homily, children hear this story, then create a "tree" illustrating the "good fruit" we bear for Jesus.

Materials

Bible
large, bare tree branch
bucket or can
sand
fruit shapes cut from heavy, colored construction paper
colored felt markers or crayons
Christmas ornament hangers
hole puncher
scissors

Before the homily fill the bucket or can with sand; anchor the branch in the sand. Cut out fruit shapes from colored construction paper, one for each child. Punch a hole at the top of each fruit shape and insert an ornament hanger through the hole.

Homily

Invite the children to come forward for today's homily. Ask them to sit in a semicircle around you.

Hold the Bible open to the Gospel of Luke as you tell today's story:

Jesus' friends sat around him on the hillside. It had been a long day. Many of them felt thirsty and hungry. Still, they listened carefully. Jesus spoke for God, and they wanted to hear every word.

"God loves everyone," Jesus said, "even the poor, the sad, the people other people don't like.

"Love as God loves. Love your enemies and be kind to them.

"Don't judge others. We all make mistakes, so stop making other people feel bad about their mistakes."

Then Jesus pointed to a nearby tree. Everyone looked at the

37

tree. It was covered with ripe fruit, ready for picking. The fruit looked delicious to Jesus' hungry friends. Jesus said, "A good tree does not give us bad fruit. A good tree gives us good fruit. You are my followers; you are to be like good trees, giving good fruit."

Several of his friends looked puzzled. "How do we give good fruit, Jesus? We're not trees!"

Jesus smiled. "I know you're not trees," he said, "but you are my followers, and as a good tree gives good fruit, my followers do good things for others."

"Oh," said one woman. "Good things like loving everyone as God loves everyone, right?"

"Right," said Jesus.

"And even loving our enemies and being good to them, right?"

"Right," Jesus said.

"And not judging people when they make mistakes, right?"

"Right," Jesus said. "Good trees give good fruit."

Discuss:
- What did Jesus say about good fruit?
- Jesus is talking about how we live our lives.
  — What do you think Jesus means by "good fruit"?
  — What "good fruit" do we see in our lives?

Distribute one fruit shape to each child. Ask the children, one at a time, to hang their fruit on the tree as each names one "good fruit" that we might see in our lives. For the benefit of the parishioners, repeat what children say if they speak quietly. Allow children who do not wish to speak aloud to hang their fruit in silence.

Prayer
- Jesus, help us to give good fruit for you. *Amen.*

Thank the children for joining you and invite them to return to their seats.

Luke 6:46-49

**"Anyone who comes to me and listens to my words and obeys them...
He is like a man who, in building his house, dug deep and laid the foundation on rock." (Luke 6:47a, 48a, *Today's English Version*)**

Summary

In this reading from the Gospel of Luke, Jesus explains that listening to and obeying him is like building a house on a firm, stable foundation. In today's homily, children listen to the story as you illustrate it with a house of cards and a house of building blocks.

Materials

Bible
playing cards (or other flimsy building material)
plastic building blocks (or other sturdy building material)

Note: If you know how to build a house of cards, use this skill as a visual focus for today's story: build the weak house from cards and the strong house from blocks, preferably interlocking plastic blocks. If you don't know how to build with cards, substitute another flimsy material—such as cardboard tubes, pieces of cardboard or notched index cards. No matter what materials you use, you may want to save time during the homily by partially assembling both structures **before the homily.**

Homily

Invite the children to come forward for today's homily. Ask them to sit in a semicircle around you.

Hold the Bible open to the Gospel of Luke as you tell today's story:

Jesus told a story:

Once there were two men. "I'm going to build a house," said one of the men.

"Me too!" said the other man.

"I want a house to play in," said the first man.

"Me, too!" said the other man.

"I want a house to sleep in," said the first man.

"Me, too!" said the other man.

"So I'm going to build my house very carefully," said the first man. "I'll start with a strong wall on a big rock. And I will work a long, long time." *(Begin to build a simple, sturdy structure using the plastic building blocks.)*

"Not me!" said the other. "I want my house now!" And he built his house as fast he could. *(Quickly build a flimsy house of cards or cardboard tubes.)* He played in his house. He slept in his house.

But the first man worked and worked, until finally his strong house was finished. *(Finish building the sturdy house.)*

Then came a terrible storm. The wind blew. *(Invite children to make the sound of wind blowing.)* Rains poured down. *(Invite children to make the motion of rain falling.)* The waters of the river rose and rose until finally they flooded the land.

Whoosh! One house was swept away. *(Knock or blow down the house of cards or cardboard tubes.)* But the house built on rock stayed forever.

Jesus said, "If you listen to my words and follow me, you're like people who carefully build sturdy homes on solid ground."

Prayer

■ Jesus, help us to listen to and follow you, so that our lives will be like strong, sturdy houses. *Amen.*

Thank the children for joining you and invite them to return to their seats.

40

Luke 7:1-10

**Jesus was surprised when he heard
this; he turned around and said to
the crowd following him, "I tell you,
I have never found faith like this,
not even in Israel!" (Luke 7:9,
Today's English Version)**

Summary

In this reading from the Gospel of
Luke, Jesus heals a Roman officer's
servant. In today's homily, children
participate in the telling of this
story, then pray for sick friends and
family members.

Homily

Invite the children to come forward
for today's homily. Ask them to sit in
a semicircle around you.

To begin the homily, teach children
the following rhythmic response, to
be said in unison when indicated in
the story. Stress the bold-faced
words or syllables. Children could
also clap in rhythm as the response
is said:

> Jesus, **heal** the **sick** to**day!**
> **Help** to **make** them **bet-ter!**
> Jesus, **heal** the **sick** to**day!**
> **Help** to **make** them **bet-ter!**

Hold the Bible open to the Gospel
of Luke as you tell today's story:

Once there was a centurion, a
soldier in the Roman army. The
centurion had a servant he
loved very much.

One day, that servant got sick,
so sick that the centurion was
afraid he might die. The centurion called his messengers. "Go
find Jesus," he said. "Ask him to
make my servant better."
(Repeat response.)

The messengers hurried down
the road. There was Jesus, talking with his disciples. "Jesus,"
called the messengers, "help us."

Jesus turned. "What do you
want?" he asked.

"Our master's servant is very
sick and about to die. Our master loves him very much. Will
you come and heal him?"
(Repeat response.)

"Certainly," said Jesus. And
immediately he began to walk
to the centurion's house. But
before he got there, more messengers came.

"Jesus, our master says not to
come to the house!" said these
messengers.

"What!" said Peter. "Doesn't
your master want the servant
cured?"

"He does," said one of the messengers. "But he also says this." And the messenger read this message:

Jesus, I am a centurion, in charge of many soldiers. When I tell a soldier to go, he goes. When I tell a soldier to come, he comes. I know that you have more power than I do. If you tell this disease to go, it will go. *(Repeat response.)*

The messenger stopped reading. Jesus said, "This centurion has faith! This centurion really trusts in God's power!" Then he said to the messengers, "Go back home. You will find the servant is all better." *(Repeat response.)*

So the messengers went home and found just what Jesus had promised. *(Repeat response.)*

Prayer

Ask the children if they know anyone who is sick. After each name is mentioned, simply pray:
■ Jesus, please heal *(repeat the name given)*.

If no sick people are named (or only a few), ask the children to name people who are well. After each name, pray:
■ Jesus, thank you for the health of *(repeat the name given)*.

Thank the children for joining you and invite them to return to their seats.

Luke 7:11-17

Then he walked over and touched the coffin, and the men carrying it stopped. Jesus said, "Young man! Get up, I tell you!" The dead man sat up and began to talk... (Luke 7:14-15a, *Today's English Version*)

Summary

In this reading from the Gospel of Luke, Jesus raises from death the son of a widow. In today's homily, children participate in a rhymed version of the story.

Materials

Bible

Note: Today's story is about the death and resurrection of a young boy. The story may raise questions about death in some children. Answer such questions with simple, honest answers. Don't tell children more than they ask to know.

Homily

Invite the children to come forward for today's homily. Ask them to sit in a semicircle around you.

Before beginning the story, invite the children to join you in doing the motions throughout. Tell the story slowly, giving children plenty of time to respond with the appropriate motions.

Hold the Bible open to the Gospel of Luke as you tell today's story:

A woman has a son who dies.
(Hold arms down, at sides. Close eyes.)

She feels so sad she cries and cries.
(Hold fists under eyes.)

Lots of people gather 'round—
(Hold arms out to embrace children seated close to you.)

All her friends from 'cross the town.
(Wave arm broadly to indicate parishioners seated in church.)

Together to the grave they walk.
(Walk fingers of one hand on palm of other hand.)

No one laughs and no one talks.
(Put finger to lips; show sad expression.)

Jesus sees them passing by,
(Place flattened hand above the eyes, as if looking in the distance.)

43

Hears her sighing, sees her cry.
(Cup hand behind ear; touch finger next to eye.)

Jesus moves to stand nearby,
(Shift position to sit closer to one child.)

To the woman, says, "Don't cry,"
(Look at the child as you say words Don't cry.*)*

Reaches out to touch the boy,
(Reach hand out into center of semicircle.)

Whispers to him, "Time for joy,"
(Cup hands around mouth as if whispering.)

Then says aloud, "Get up, young man!
(Raise right hand, palm up.)

Come to life. It's my command!"
(Raise left hand, palm up.)

People gasp, they jump, they hide;
(Hide face behind hands.)

The boy sits up; he is alive!
(Drop hands; sit up tall and strong.)

"Who is this man?" a woman asks.

"He gives back life—no simple task!"
(Hold hands out and to sides, questioningly; raise shoulders.)

Another says, "He heals the sick.

(Rest hands lightly and briefly on the heads of two or three children.)

He teaches well and answers quick."
(Hold hands out, palms up, as if holding an open book.)

A man chimes in, "He calms the storm!
(Move hands side to side, palms down, as if smoothing rough water.)

Could he be God in human form?
(Put single finger to side of forehead, questioning.)

Whatever else you think or say,
(Point at each child, individually.)

God has come to us today!"
(Place hands, one on top of the other, over your heart.)

If you wish, discuss with the children:
- What happened to the boy at the *beginning* of today's story?
- How did the boy's mother feel at that time?
- What happened to the boy at the *end* of today's story?
- How did the boy's mother feel then?

Prayer

- Dear Jesus, thank you for giving life to the boy who died. *Amen.*

Thank the children for joining you and invite them to return to their seats.

Luke 7:36-50

"I tell you, then, the great love she has shown proves that her many sins have been forgiven. But whoever has been forgiven little shows only a little love." (Luke 7:47, _Today's English Version_)

Summary

In this reading from the Gospel of Luke, a woman demonstrates her deep love for Jesus by anointing his feet with perfume. In today's homily, children first share stories about "doing something wrong," then hear the message of forgiveness in today's story.

Materials

Bible

Today's homily invites you to share with the children a brief account of a time you were forgiven for something you did that was wrong. This may be a story you want to think about and prepare **before the homily**. Although children will relate well to a story about your childhood, consider sharing a story from your adult life. Children need to realize that "doing something wrong" is not an experience confined to childhood.

Homily

Invite the children to come forward for today's homily. Ask them to sit in a semicircle around you.

Begin the homily by sharing the story about personal wrong-doing that you prepared **before the homily**.

Invite children to share their own stories, thoughts and feelings, too. Conclude this time of sharing by saying:
■ A woman once said she was sorry in a very special way, and that's the story I want to tell you today.

Hold the Bible open to the Gospel of Luke as you tell today's story:

Once there was a woman who did something wrong. "I wish I hadn't done that," said the woman. "I feel so bad."

Then the woman heard good news. "Jesus is in our town," she heard. "Jesus is eating at Simon's house."

The woman got up. She went to buy a costly bottle of fine perfume. Then she took the bottle and walked to Simon's house.

She opened the door. Simon was sitting at his table, eating. Jesus was sitting at the table, eating. Many other people were eating, too.

The woman didn't wait for a minute. She went right to Jesus. And then she knelt down in front of him and began to cry.

The woman's tears ran all over Jesus' feet—so she dried them with her hair. She kissed his feet, and poured her best perfume all over them.

Jesus looked at her and said, "You love me very much, don't you?"

"Yes," the woman said.

"Don't worry," said Jesus. "I know you are sorry for what you did. And I forgive you."

If you wish, discuss with the children:
■ How do you think the woman feels after she is forgiven?
■ What do you imagine the woman says to her friends? her family?
■ How have we felt after someone has forgiven us?
■ How have we felt after we have forgiven someone else?

Prayer
■ Jesus, thank you for forgiving each one of us. *Amen.*

Thank the children for joining you and invite them to return to their seats.

Luke 9:18-24

And he said to them all, "If you want to come with me, you must forget yourself, take up your cross every day, and follow me." (Luke 9:23, *Today's English Version***)**

Summary

In this reading from the Gospel of Luke, Jesus first asks the disciples who they think he is, then urges them to take up their crosses and follow him. In today's homily, children learn to sing a simple story refrain, sing the refrain as they participate in the story, and talk briefly about ways to follow Jesus.

Materials

Bible

Homily

Invite the children to come forward for today's homily. Ask them to sit in a semicircle around you.

Begin the homily by teaching the children (and the parishioners) this simple refrain, sung to the tune of "It's Raining, It's Pouring":

> O come, follow Jesus.
> Come now and follow Jesus.

Invite the children (and the parishioners) to sing this refrain when indicated in the story.

Hold the Bible open to the Gospel of Luke as you tell today's story:

One day Jesus was all alone, praying. His disciples came to him. His disciples came every day because they wanted to learn how to: *(Sing refrain.)*

"Who do people say I am?" asked Jesus.

"Some say you are John, the man who baptized people in the river," said one disciple.

"Some say you are Elijah, the prophet who went to heaven in a chariot of fire," said another disciple.

"Some say you are a prophet who died and came back to life," said a third disciple.

"And who do *you* think I am?" asked Jesus.

"You are the one God sent to us," said Peter. "God wants us to:" *(Sing refrain.)*

"Yes," said Jesus. "I am the one God has sent. But I have hard days ahead. I will carry a cross. I will die on that cross. Some people will kill me, because they don't know that God wants them to:" *(Sing refrain.)*

47

"But three days after I die, God will give me new life," said Jesus.

"Will we know you again?" asked a disciple.

"Yes," said Jesus. "You will always be able to know me. You will always be able to:" *(Sing refrain.)*

"Will it be easy to follow you?" asked a disciple.

"No," said Jesus. "It will be as hard as carrying a heavy cross. But if you can follow me, you will be glad. You will live with me forever if you:" *(Sing refrain.)*

With the children, discuss:
- I wonder: Why does Jesus want us to follow him?
- In what ways do we follow Jesus?
  — When is it fun to follow Jesus?
  — When is it hard to follow Jesus?

Prayer
- Jesus, thank you for inviting us to follow you. Help us to follow you every day. *Amen.*

Thank the children for joining you and invite them to return to their seats.

48

Luke 9:28-36

While he was praying, his face changed its appearance, and his clothes became dazzling white. (Luke 9:29, *Today's English Version*)

Summary

In this reading from the Gospel of Luke, Jesus is transfigured on the mountaintop. In today's homily, children hear this story, then either join you in an action rhyme of today's story *or* affirm what God's power can do.

Materials

Bible

Homily

Invite the children to come forward for today's homily. Ask them to sit in a semicircle around you.

Hold the Bible open to the Gospel of Luke as you tell today's story:

"Let's go for a walk, friends," says Jesus.

"I'll come," says Peter.

"I'll come," says John.

"I'll come," says James.

Jesus and his friends walk to the mountains. They climb up and up—all the way up to the top of a mountain.

"I want to pray," says Jesus.

He lifts his arms and prays.

"Look!" says Peter.

"Jesus shines!" says John.

"Jesus dazzles!" says James.

A cloud covers the mountain. Peter, James and John hear a voice from the cloud.

"Jesus is my dear Son," says the voice. "Listen to Jesus."

"I'll listen," says Peter.

"I'll listen," says James.

"I'll listen," says John.

The cloud goes away. Jesus and his friends walk back down the mountain.

Peter thinks, "I'm glad I was with Jesus."

James thinks, "I'm glad I saw Jesus dazzle."

John thinks, "I'm glad I saw what God's power can do."

Option 1
Invite the children to learn a rhymed version of today's story. Begin by standing in a circle with the children. Teach children the words and movements to this story:

We are climbing
Up with Jesus,
Up the hill,
A long, long way.
(Circle to the right, making climbing motions with your feet and hands.)

When we reach the top,
We're tired,
(Hold back of hand to forehead.)
So we sleep
(Pillow head on hands.)
while Jesus prays.
(Fold hands to pray.)

When we wake,
We look at Jesus.
(Shade eyes with hand.)
Jesus shines
As bright as light.
(Thumbs beside eyes, spread out fingers.)

"Listen to my
Son," says God.
(Cup ear with hand.)
"My Son will teach
you what is right."
(Extend arms to front, palms up.)

Option 2:
Ask the children:
■ What do you think God's power can do?

Affirm as many of the children's answers as possible with a thanksgiving to God. For example, if a child says, "Make Jesus dazzle!" you can respond, "Thank you, God, for making Jesus dazzle."

Prayer

■ Thank you, God, for making Jesus dazzle. Thank you for telling Jesus' friends to listen to Jesus. Thank you for all that your power can do. *Amen.*

Thank the children for joining you and invite them to return to their seats.

Luke 9:51-62

Jesus said to him, "Foxes have holes, and birds have nests, but the Son of Man has no place to lie down and rest." (Luke 9:58, *Today's English Version*)

Summary

In this reading from the Gospel of Luke, Jesus warns would-be followers that discipleship requires sacrifice. In today's homily, children first discuss "excuses," then hear and talk about the excuses for not following Jesus given in today's story.

Materials

Bible
large poster board titled *Excuses! Excuses!*
felt marker

Homily

Invite the children to come forward for today's homily. Ask them to sit in a semicircle around you.

Begin by offering a variety of "excuses" related to today's homily; for example:
■ Well, you know, I meant to sing a special song for you today, but I lost my music.
■ And I had intended to bake cookies for us, but I was just too tired last night.
■ And I prepared a wonderful special homily to share with you, but my dog ate my notes.

Pause for a few seconds and then ask:
■ What am I doing? What do we call it when we give reasons why we didn't or can't do something? *(making excuses)*

Direct children's attention to the large sheet of newsprint or butcher paper titled *Excuses! Excuses!* Ask:
■ What is an excuse?
■ What are some of our favorite excuses? What excuses do we use when we don't want to go to bed? when we don't want to brush our teeth? when we don't want to go to school?

Invite a helper to write the children's answers to this final question on the poster board.

Hold the Bible open to the Gospel of Luke as you tell today's story:

One day Jesus was walking along a road. Men followed Jesus. Women followed Jesus. Children followed Jesus. They all wanted to follow Jesus.

One man walked up to Jesus and said, "I will follow you wherever you go."

But Jesus said, "You might not find a place to sleep! Foxes have holes to sleep in. Birds have nests to sleep in. But I don't have any place at all."

No place to sleep! Sounds like it's hard to follow Jesus!

Another man came to Jesus and said, "I want to follow you, but my father has just died. Shouldn't I go home and help my family bury my father first?"

But Jesus said, "No, no excuses. Let your family bury your father. You come and follow me."

A third man came to Jesus and said, "I want to follow you. But shouldn't I go say good-bye to my family first?"

But Jesus said, "No, no excuses. Don't wait another minute. Right now, come, and follow me."

A woman came to Jesus and said, "I want to follow you. But I need to finish gathering the grain from my fields. Shouldn't I take care of that first?"

But Jesus said, "No, no excuses. Your friends and family will bring in the grain. Come, now, and follow me."

With the children, discuss:
- In today's story, people give excuses for not following Jesus. What excuses did we hear?
- What other excuses do we use when we don't want to follow Jesus? What excuses do we use when we don't want to share? when we don't want to listen? when we don't want to help?

Ask the older child to add the children's answers to this last question to the poster board.

In conclusion, discuss:
- How can we follow Jesus without excuses?

Prayer

- Jesus, help us to let go of our excuses and to follow you. *Amen.*

Thank the children for joining you and invite them to return to their seats.

Luke 10: 1-12, 16-20

After this the Lord chose another seventy-two men and sent them out two by two, to go ahead of him to every town and place where he himself was about to go. (Luke 10:1, *Today's English Version***)**

Summary

In this reading from the Gospel of Luke, Jesus sends out pairs of friends to teach and heal. In today's homily, children play a game of Simon Says, hear today's story and discuss "who's in charge."

Materials

Bible

Homily

Invite the children to come forward for today's homily. Ask them to sit in a semicircle around you.

Begin today's homily with a brief game of Simon Says. You could, for example, offer these directions to children:
- Simon says, stand up.
- Simon says, wave your arms over your head.
- Jump up and down. *(Oops! Simon did not say to do this one!)*
- Simon says, whisper your name.
- Simon says, sit down.

After children are seated, discuss:
- In the game of Simon Says, who's in charge?
- How about at your house? Who's in charge there?
- Who's in charge at your school?
- Who's in charge here today?
- What does it mean to be in charge?
- Someone's in charge in today's story. See if you can figure out who it is.

Hold the Bible open to the Gospel of Luke as you tell today's story:

"Come, friends," called Jesus. "I have good news for you today."

The friends of Jesus came running: two friends, twelve friends, thirty friends, sixty friends—seventy-two friends in all!

"Here we are, Jesus," said the friends. "What do you want?"

"Go where I send you," said Jesus.

"Where will you send us?" said the friends.

"I will send you, two by two. I will send you to heal the sick. I will send you to tell people good news. I will send you to tell people that God's kingdom is near."

And out went Jesus' friends, into the world, two by two. They healed the sick. They told people good news. They told people that God's kingdom was near.

Then, two by two, the seventy-two friends came back to Jesus.

"Jesus," the friends called. "We have done your work. Even demons ran away when we did your work!"

"Welcome, friends," said Jesus. "And be glad: God's kingdom is near, and you will be God's friends forever."

With the children, discuss:
- In today's gospel story, who is in charge?
- What happens when Jesus is in charge?
- Because Jesus is in charge, he invites us to tell others about God's love.
- How can we tell others about God's great love?

Repeat the game of "Simon Says," this time using the following directions:
- Simon says, tell the children next to you that God loves them very much!
- Simon says, tell the children next to you, "God's kingdom is here!"
- Simon says, let's all say, "God takes care of me!"
- Simon says, give someone in the church a hug.
- Simon says, let's all say to the church, "I'll follow Jesus!"
- Simon says, let's have everyone in church shout "Amen!"

Prayer
- Jesus, we pray for all your friends. Help all your friends, including each one of us, to tell others about you. *Amen.*

Thank the children for joining you and invite them to return to their seats.

Luke 10:25-37

"But a Samaritan who was traveling that way came upon the man, and when he saw him, his heart was filled with pity." (Luke 10:33, *Today's English Version***)**

Summary

In this reading from the Gospel of Luke, Jesus answers the teacher's question, "Who is my neighbor?" with the story of the good Samaritan. In today's homily, children identify each other as neighbors, hear today's story and discuss ways to be neighbors to each other.

Materials

Bible
poster board on which you have written the question *Who is my neighbor?*

Homily

Invite the children to come forward for today's homily. Ask them to stand in pairs in a circle with you.

Call out simple commands that include the word *neighbor*; for example:
■ Hug your neighbor.
■ Touch your neighbor's toes.
■ Shake hands with your neighbor.
■ Tell your neighbor your name.

Older children might enjoy taking turns giving simple "neighbor" commands.

After a minute or two, ask children to sit in a semicircle around you. Say:
■ Jesus once told a story about being neighbors, and that's the story I want to tell you today.

Hold the Bible open to the Gospel of Luke as you tell today's story:

One day a man was traveling from Jerusalem to Jericho. Suddenly, from out of nowhere, a band of robbers jumped on the man. The robbers stole all his clothes and all his money. They beat the man and left him on the road to die.

Now on that same road were other travelers. And soon one of these travelers, a priest, came walking down the road. He saw the wounded man, but he did not go to him. He hurried away.

Another traveler came—a Levite, who served God in the holy temple in Jerusalem. But he did not stop. He saw the wounded man and hurried away.

Then came a third traveler, a stranger from the land of Samaria. He saw the wounded man, but he did not hurry away. "What is this?" he said, and ran to the side of the wounded man. The stranger knelt down and put his warm cloak over the man.

"This man needs medicine, right away," said the stranger. So he opened his bag and took out wine and oil to put on the man's wounds. The stranger wrapped bandages on the wounds, then took the man to an inn to rest.

"Who is this?" said the innkeeper.

"I do not know," said the stranger. "But take care of him. Here is money to pay you what it will cost to feed him. I will be back again, and if you need more money, just tell me. But let him live here until he is all better."

"Well, you may not know who he is," said the innkeeper. "But I know who you are. You are this man's friend. You are this man's neighbor."

Show the poster board on which you have written the question:
■ Who is my neighbor?

Ask an older child to read this question aloud. Then discuss:
■ What is a neighbor?
■ Who are our neighbors?
■ Who was the good neighbor in today's story?
■ What did the good neighbor do to help the man who was hurt?
■ Who have been good neighbors to us?
■ When have we been good neighbors to people who were hurting?
■ How can we be good neighbors for people we know? How can we help someone who is hurt? lonely? sad? frightened?

Prayer

■ Jesus, help us to be good neighbors for people we know who are sad, sick, lonely or hurting. *Amen.*

Thank the children for joining you and invite them to return to their seats.

56

Luke 10:38-42

The Lord answered her, "Martha, Martha! You are worried and troubled over so many things, but just one is needed. Mary has chosen the right thing, and it will not be taken away from her." (Luke 10:41-42, *Today's English Version***)**

Summary

In this reading from the Gospel of Luke, Jesus encourages Martha to release her busyness and join her sister Mary as she listens to Jesus' teaching—to *do* less and *be* more. In today's homily, children hear the story, then act it out together.

Materials

Bible

Homily

Invite the children to come forward for today's homily. Ask them to sit in a semicircle around you.

Hold the Bible open to the Gospel of Luke as you tell today's story:

Jesus traveled from town to town. One day, he traveled to the house of two friends. These friends were sisters, named Mary and Martha. When Jesus came to the door, Mary and Martha were glad to see him. "Welcome, Jesus," they said.

Jesus came in and sat down.

Martha ran to get water for Jesus to drink. Mary sat at Jesus' feet, listening to Jesus talk.

Martha set the pitcher of water near Jesus. Then she ran back to the kitchen to get food for Jesus. Mary sat at his feet.

Martha brought out bread for Jesus to eat. Mary sat at his feet.

Martha brought out fresh cheese for Jesus to eat. Mary sat at his feet.

Martha brought out dried fruit for Jesus to eat. Mary sat at his feet.

Martha was angry. "Jesus," she said. "Don't you care that my sister is just sitting there while I do all this work? Make her help me!"

"Martha," said Jesus. "You are very busy. You have brought me many things—but I only need one thing from you. Mary has chosen the best thing to do, and she can stay right here with me."

Invite the children to reenact the story of Jesus, Mary and Martha as you retell it.

Supplement the story by describing what Martha might have been doing in the kitchen, for example, chopping vegetables, washing up the dishes, setting the table, etc. You can also ask the children to suggest what else Martha might have been doing. Act these out together.

When you relate Mary's part in the story, offer suggested ways that Mary was showing her interest in Jesus and what he was saying. For example, she looked at him as he talked, she nodded when she agreed with him, she rested a hand on his arm when she had a question, etc. Again, ask the children to suggest other ways in which Mary showed her interest. Act these out together.

Invite the children to say in unison with Martha:
■ Jesus, make Mary help me!

Ask:
■ How does Jesus answer?
■ What nice things was Martha doing for Jesus?
■ What one other thing do you think Jesus invited Martha to do?
■ What do you think Mary heard when she listened to Jesus?
■ How can we listen to Jesus today?

Prayer
■ Jesus, help us to listen to you. *Amen.*

Thank the children for joining you and invite them to return to their seats.

58

Luke 11:1-13

"And so I say to you: Ask, and you will receive; seek, and you will find; knock, and the door will be opened to you." (Luke 11:9, _Today's English Version_)

Summary

In this reading from the Gospel of Luke, Jesus teaches his followers about prayer. In today's homily, children join in the telling of the story, then offer "knocking" prayers to God.

Materials

Bible
hard surfaces on which to knock (see **note** below)

Note: In the today's story and the prayer that follows, children are invited to knock. If the floor on which you gather is hard (wood or tile) children can knock directly on the floor. If the floor is carpeted, bring in items with hard surfaces (blocks of wood, boards, etc.) on which children can knock. Bring enough items so each child can easily reach a hard, knockable surface.

Homily

Invite the children to come forward for today's homily. Ask them to sit in a semicircle around you.

Begin by sharing a few knock-knock jokes with children. At the beginning of each joke, when you say "knock, knock," invite children to knock twice on the floor or boards.

Leader: Knock, knock!
Children: Who's there?
Leader: Isabelle.
Children: Isabelle who?
Leader: Isabelle necessary on a bicycle?

Leader: Knock, knock!
Children: Who's there?
Leader: Ivan.
Children: Ivan who?
Leader: Ivan to come in; it's cold out here.

Leader: Knock, knock!
Children: Who's there?
Leader: Tonya.
Children: Tonya who?
Leader: Tonya want to see for yourself?

Children may have their own knock-knock jokes to share.

After sharing several jokes, say:
- Today's story tells us something about knocking, too.
- Every time I say the word _knock_, knock twice on the floor (or boards).

Hold the Bible open to the Gospel of Luke as you tell today's story:

One night, a man was sitting in his house when a knock *(children knock)* came at the door. "I wonder who that could be?" the man said. He opened the door. There was an old friend, who lived far away.

"Welcome, friend," said the man. He brought his friend inside. "I'm so glad to see you. Sit down and let me get you some food."

But when the man went to the kitchen, he found nothing to eat. "Uh, oh," said the man. "No food. What will I give my friend?"

The man slipped out the door and ran to his neighbor's house. He knocked *(children knock)* at his neighbor's door.

"What do you want?" said the sleepy neighbor.

"Food!" said the man. "A friend has come to see me and I have no food to give him."

"No!" yelled the neighbor. "It's late! Go away!"

But the man knocked *(children knock)* harder.

"Now what?" called the neighbor.

"Please," said the man. "I need food for my friend."

"Listen," said the neighbor. "My house is locked. My children are asleep. Go away!"

But the man knocked *(children knock)* harder. And harder. And harder.

Until finally the neighbor yelled, "All right! Just a minute! And I will give you what you want!"

Jesus told this story a long time ago. Afterward, Jesus said, "Ask, and you will receive. Seek, and you will find. Knock, and the door will be opened."

Prayer

Invite the children to offer "knocking" prayers. Each child who wants to pray knocks twice on the floor or on a board, then tells God what is on his or her mind.

After all children who wish to do so have knocked and prayed, knock twice yourself and pray:
- Dear God, thanks for promising that you always hear us when we pray. *Amen.*

Thank the children for joining you and invite them to return to their seats.

Luke 12:13-31

Then Jesus said to the disciples, "And so I tell you not to worry about the food you need to stay alive or about the clothes you need for your body."
(Luke 12:22, *Today's English Version*)

Summary

In this reading from the Gospel of Luke, Jesus helps his followers deal with their fear of the future by telling the parable of the rich fool. In today's homily, children hear this story, then share their worries and discuss trusting in God.

Materials

Bible
large poster board on which you have drawn the outline of a barn (see diagram below)
felt marker

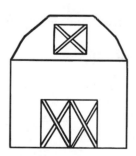

Homily

Invite the children to come forward for today's homily. Ask them to sit in a semicircle around you.

Hold the Bible open to the Gospel of Luke as you tell today's story:

Jesus overheard some of his friends talking. One man said, "I'm low on money, and soon I'll need some new clothes. How will I get them?"

A woman added, "We've gone all day without eating. I'm very hungry. Where will we find food to eat?"

The woman's daughter asked, "It's too cold to sleep outside tonight. Where will we find shelter?"

Jesus felt sad for his friends who worried so much: What will they wear? What will they eat? Where will they sleep? So Jesus said, "Let me tell you a story:

"Once a man planted a field. He tilled the ground. He made the ground nice and soft.

"He sowed the seeds. He scattered the seeds all over the ground.

"He watered the seeds. He gave the seeds water to drink.

"He watched the plants grow. He pulled out the weeds.

'Look at this food grow!' the man said. 'I have wheat! I have corn! I have grapes! I have figs! I have more food than I've ever had before!'

"Then came the time to gather the food. 'First I'll gather wheat,' he said, so he gathered and gathered and gathered wheat.

"'Now I'll gather my corn,' he said, and he gathered and gathered and gathered corn.

"'Now I'll gather my grapes,' he said, and he gathered and gathered and gathered grapes.

"'Now I'll gather my figs,' he said, and he gathered and gathered and gathered figs.

"'Look at all my food!' he said. 'I have enough food to eat for years! Now I'll do nothing but eat my food!'

"But that very night, the man died. He had to leave his food behind. And he never ate one bite."

"Is that the end of the story, Jesus?" asked the woman.

"Yes."

"I don't get it," said the man.

Jesus continued: "Don't you understand how much God loves us? God will make sure we have enough to eat. God will make sure we have clothes to wear. God will make sure we have a place to sleep."

Jesus looked around at his friends. "Trust in God," he said.

Discuss with the children:
■ What do we worry about?

As children share their worries, write or draw each one on the poster board within the outline of the barn. After all who wish to share have done so, continue:
■ What does worrying feel like?
■ Who helps us when we worry?
■ Jesus invites us to worry less and trust God more. How do you think we can do that?

Prayer

Pray aloud for each item written or drawn on the barn poster. You could, for example, use any or all of these prayer forms:
■ God, please help us with...
■ Dear God, help us to worry less about...
■ God, thank you for helping us with...
■ God, we trust you with...

Close by praying:
■ Dear God, thank you for helping us with all the things we worry about. *Amen.*

Thank the children for joining you and invite them to return to their seats.

Luke 13:6-9

Then Jesus told them this parable: "There was once a man who had a fig tree growing in his vineyard. He went looking for figs on it but found none." (Luke 13:6, *Today's English Version*)

Summary

In this reading from the Gospel of Luke, Jesus illustrates God's grace and patience with the parable of the unfruitful fig tree. In today's homily, children first discuss what trees need to grow, then hear the story and talk about ways in which they are nurtured by those who love them.

Materials

Bible
large, healthy, tree-like potted plant

Homily

Invite the children to come forward for today's homily. Ask them to sit in a semicircle around you.

Place the potted plant in the middle of the semicircle. Ask the children:
- What is *this?*
- What can we do to help this tree grow strong and healthy? *(Give it sunshine, water and fertilizer; keep it clean and free of bugs and disease; care for it.)*
- Jesus once told a story about

caring for a tree, and that's the story I want to tell you today.

You may wish to move the tree out of the semicircle before beginning the story. Hold the Bible open to the Gospel of Luke as you tell today's story:

Once there was a man who owned a vineyard, filled with grapevines. He loved to walk through the vineyard as the sun was setting, smelling the sweet grapes that hung heavy on the vines, feeling the first cool evening breeze on his skin.

In the middle of his vineyard was a large, old fig tree. One evening, as the owner of the vineyard strolled among the grapes, he stopped in the center of the vineyard to check on the old fig tree. He squinted up into the tree. "Where are the figs?" he asked aloud, not realizing that the gardener was just around on the other side of the tree.

"There are no figs," the tree said...or at least, the owner

thought the tree said it, but really it was the gardener.

The gardener walked around the tree. The owner looked annoyed. "Year after year this tree stands here," said the owner crossly, "and year after year it never gives any figs. What good is it? Chop it down!"

Silently, the gardener put his hand out and rested it on the trunk of the old tree. He felt the rough bark; he looked up and saw the golden sun fading from the top leaves of the tree.

"Sir," said the gardener, "let the tree alone for one more year. I will care for it. I will water it. I will fertilize it. I will prune it. I will make sure it gets rinsed with the rain and warmed by the bright sun. Then, next year, it will give us good fruit."

The owner watched the gardener. He loves this old tree, thought the owner. "Okay," he said. "Take care of the tree. And next year? *Figs!*"

Place the potted tree back in the center of the semicircle of children. Say:
■ Let's pretend this is the fig tree in today's story. Can we all help care for it?
■ Let's water the fig tree. (*Invite the children to pretend to water that tree.*)
■ Let's feed the fig tree some rich fertilizer. (*Invite the children to pretend to mix fertilizer at the base of the tree.*)

■ Let's pretend to cut off the old, dying branches so new, living branches can grow. (*Invite the children to pretend to prune branches.*)
■ Let's pretend to be rain washing the fig tree clean. (*Invite the children to "rain" on the tree.*)
■ Let's pretend to be sunshine, bright and warm, all over the fig tree's green leaves. (*Invite the children to "shine" on the tree.*)
■ Now let's stand back and watch. Do you see figs growing on the tree. (*Pretend to see figs, first a few, then many, covering the tree.*)

Move the tree outside of the semicircle once again; ask the children to be seated. Discuss:
■ What do *we* need to grow? (*Encourage a variety of responses.*)
■ Who gives us what we need to grow?
■ In Jesus' story, the fig tree got a second chance. Who in our lives has given us second chances? Can you tell us about those times?

Prayer

■ Dear God, thanks for helping us to grow strong and healthy, like the fig tree. Thanks for giving us second chances, too. *Amen.*

Thank the children for joining you and invite them to return to their seats.

Luke 13:22-30

"People will come from the east and the west, from the north and the south, and sit down at the feast in the Kingdom of God." (Luke 13:29, *Today's English Version*)

Summary

In this reading from the Gospel of Luke, Jesus invites his followers to feast in the kingdom of God. In today's homily, children share about parties, hear today's story and imagine what a party in God's kingdom might be like.

Materials

Bible
assorted party goods: tablecloth, candles, balloons, party favors, snacks, etc.

Before the homily use the assorted party goods to decorate the space in which the children will gather for the homily.

Homily

Invite the children to come forward for today's homily. Ask them to sit in a semicircle around you.

Begin by directing children's attention to the party decorations. Ask:
- What's all this?
- When was the last time you went to a party?
- Who was at the party?
- What did you do at the party?

- What did you eat at the party?
- Jesus once invited his followers to a party, and that's the story I want to tell you today.

Hold the Bible open to the Gospel of Luke as you tell today's story:

One day, Jesus said to his friends, "I want you to come to my party."

"A party!" said his friends. "Where will it be?"

"In the kingdom of God," said Jesus.

"Who can come?" said the friends.

"Many people will come," said Jesus. "People will come from the North to my party. People will come from the South to my party. People will come from the East to my party. People will come from the West to my party."

"How do we get there?" said the friends.

"You must go in through the narrow door," said Jesus. "Or

you won't be able to come in."

"You mean we can only get in through the narrow door?" asked the friends.

"That's right," said Jesus. "Some people won't go through that door, and they will stand outside, crying instead. But don't you do that! Come to my party! Go through the narrow door!"

With the children, discuss:
- Would you like to go to Jesus' party? Why or why not?
- Who else do you think will come to God's party?

- What do you think will happen at God's party?
- What would *you* like to do at God's party?

If you brought snacks for today's homily, share them with the children.

Prayer

- Jesus, thank you for inviting each child here—*(name each child, if possible)*—to your party in God's kingdom. *Amen.*

Thank the children for joining you and invite them to return to their seats.

66

Luke 14:1, 7-14

"When you give a feast, invite the poor, the crippled, the lame, and the blind; and you will be blessed, because they are not able to pay you back." (Luke 14:13-14a, *Today's English Version***)**

Summary

In this reading from the Gospel of Luke, Jesus attends a dinner party, observes the guests' behavior and teaches about humility and hospitality. In today's homily, children first hear today's story, then create a guest list for a pretend party.

Materials

Bible
sheet or poster board or newsprint
felt marker

Homily

Invite the children to come forward for today's homily. Ask them to sit in a semicircle around you.

Explain to the children:
■ In today's homily, let's pretend we're planning a party.

Direct attention to the poster board or newsprint as you write the title *Guest List* across the top. Ask a volunteer to read what you have written. Discuss:
■ What do you think we'll write on this, our guest list?
■ That's right, on our guest list we

will write the names of the people we want to invite to our party.
■ But before we make out our guest list, let's listen to a story about Jesus, when *he* went to a party.

Hold the Bible open to the Gospel of Luke as you tell today's story:

One day, Jesus was invited to a dinner party at the home of one of the religious leaders. Lots of other people were invited too. They were curious about Jesus.

"I hear his teaching is amazing," said one party guest.

"Yes," said another guest. "And I've heard he can heal people who are sick!"

As the guests arrived for the party, they kept pushing forward to try to sit close to Jesus. Everyone wanted to be near the guest of honor, to ask questions, to see what he looked like. They weren't being very polite, stepping in each other's way, elbowing each other,

telling people to get out of their way.

Jesus felt sad. So, as he often did, he started to teach:

"When you get invited to a feast, don't rush in and push your way to the front, trying to get the best seat. Don't worry if you're more important than someone else. Take a seat anywhere, and if the people giving the party want you to move to a special seat, they will ask you."

Jesus smiled. "People who try to be first all the time usually end up last!" he said. "And the last often end up first!"

Then Jesus noticed that everyone else invited to the dinner party was nicely dressed. They wore expensive jewelry. They were wealthy friends and relatives of the people giving the party. "Hmm," Jesus said. "I don't see many of the people I meet every day on the street here tonight."

Jesus felt sad again, so he taught some more:

"When you give a party, don't just invite the people you know will invite you to a party at their house. Invite the people who can't afford to give parties. Invite the people who hardly ever get invited to parties. Invite lonely people, sick people, friendless people, frightened people, poor people. They won't be able to invite you back, but God will be very pleased."

And just like every time that Jesus taught, some people listened...and some people didn't.

But Jesus enjoyed the party anyway.

Direct children's attention back to the "Guest List" started on newsprint or poster board. Ask:
■ Who did Jesus say to invite to our pretend party?

Write down all people named by the children, including, if they mention them, friends and family members. If necessary, remind children also to invite people who otherwise might not be invited to a party...the poor, the sick, the lonely, etc.

Conclude by saying:
■ This is a great party list! I think Jesus would like to come to this party!

Prayer

■ Jesus, thank you for reminding us to love all people, not just our friends and family members. *Amen.*

Thank the children for joining you and invite them to return to their seats.

Luke 14:25-33

"In the same way," Jesus concluded,
"none of you can be my disciple un-
less you give up everything you have."
(Luke 14:33, *Today's English Version*)

Summary

In this reading from the Gospel of Luke, Jesus describes the high cost of discipleship. In today's homily, children first attempt to build a tower of blocks or cards, then hear today's story.

Materials

Bible
building blocks or playing cards

Homily

Invite the children to come forward for today's homily. Ask them to sit in a semicircle around you.

Engage the children in building a tower of blocks or cards. As you work together, discuss:
- What do we need for building a tower?
- What if we only had one or two blocks (or cards), could we build a tower?
- Can we build a church or tower alone? What do we need?

Close by saying:
- In our story today, someone decides to build a tower—but without thinking first.

Hold the Bible open to the Gospel of Luke as you tell today's story:

The girl followed along with the great crowd who had come to hear Jesus. They were walking a dusty road when Jesus turned and asked, "Do you love me?"

"Yes!" they all shouted.

The girl saw Jesus smile. It felt good to be loved. The girl smiled, too.

Jesus asked, "Will you follow me?"

"Yes!" the people cried again.

Jesus spoke quietly, "Will you love me more than your father or your mother?"

The girl listened even more carefully. What did Jesus mean?

The people shook their heads, "Yes."

"Will you love me even more than your sisters or your brothers?" Jesus asked.

"Yes," they said again.

"Will you love me even more than your wife or your husband or your children?"

Now there was silence. Now the people were thinking. Jesus was serious about what he was asking.

"To be my disciple," Jesus said, "you must pick up your cross and follow me."

"To be my disciple," Jesus continued, "you must first figure out how much it will cost you.

"If you are planning to build a tower, you must first figure out what the bricks and mortar and workers will cost. If you don't, you may start the tower but run out of money before you finish it. Then people will laugh and say, 'This person began to build but now can't finish the job. Hah!'

"Will you love me," Jesus continued, "even more than you love yourself?"

The crowd was silent. Jesus waited. The girl watched.One by one people wandered away, across the fields, down the road.

They had wanted to hear what Jesus had to say, but they had not known that he would ask so much of the people who followed him.

The girl looked at Jesus, thinking about what Jesus had said. She sighed and then she smiled, as she answered, "Yes."

Prayer

■ Dear Jesus, help us to be willing to follow you, no matter what it costs. *Amen.*

Thank the children for joining you and invite them to return to their seats.

70

Luke 15:1-10

"In the same way, I tell you, the angels of God rejoice over one sin- ner who repents." (Luke 15:10, *Today's English Version***)**

Summary

In this reading from the Gospel of Luke, Jesus tells the parables of the lost sheep and the lost coin, illus- trating God's unceasing love for us. In today's homily, children first hunt for a lost coin and a lost sheep, then hear today's story.

Materials

Bible
2 bags filled with various objects, for example, clothing, books, toys, etc.
a quarter
a small plastic sheep, as found in a nativity set or a toy farm set

Before the homily hide the quar- ter at the bottom of one the bags and the plastic sheep at the bottom of the other bag.

Homily

Invite the children to come for- ward for today's homily. Ask them to sit in a semicircle around you.

Show children the two bags. Explain that you have dropped a quarter in one of the bags. Would several children help you find your lost coin?

Explain that you have lost a small plastic sheep in the other bag. Would several children help you find your lost sheep?

Give children a minute or two to find both items, then say:
■ You found a lost coin! You found a lost sheep!
■ Now listen for a lost coin and a lost sheep in today's story.

Hold the Bible open to the Gospel of Luke as you tell today's story:

Once there was a shepherd who each night counted his sheep.

One sheep! Two sheep! Ten sheep! Fifty sheep!

"...ninety-eight, ninety-nine, one hundred," said the shep- herd. "Now good night and sleep tight."

But one day the shepherd counted, "...ninety-eight, nine- ty-nine..." He stopped. "Ninety- nine? Where's my other sheep?"

The sun was setting; the evening air was cold. But the shepherd didn't wait long enough to say, "Good night,

71

sleep tight." Out he went over the fields, the hills and the rocky mountains.

He called and called. "Come to me, sheep! It's time to go home, sheep!"

Finally, in the dark night he heard a weak "baa." There was the lost sheep, wandering his own way. The shepherd put his arms around the sheep and swung it right over his shoulders, even though the sheep was heavier than any one of you!

"Now the day is a happy one," laughed the shepherd. "I've found you and we're going home."

When he got home, he shouted aloud for the whole town to hear, "Come and celebrate! Let's have a party! My sheep was lost, and now it's found!"

And once there was a woman who had ten silver coins. Each day she counted her coins

One coin! Two coins! Five coins! Ten coins!

But one day the woman counted, "...seven, eight, nine...*nine*? Where's my other coin?"

The bread needed baking and the wool needed spinning, but the woman didn't wait one minute. She took up her lamp and broom and swept the house out, making the dust fly

in every corner and peering in every nook and cranny.

All that morning she searched. Finally, in a narrow crack in the floor, her lamp struck a glint of light. The woman peered inside and scratched with her fingernail. Out came her missing silver coin.

The woman laughed so loudly that the baby tied to her back laughed, too. The woman ran into the streets and shouted aloud to her friends. "Look!" she cried. "This precious coin was lost, but I have found it! Come and celebrate! Let's have a party!"

Jesus told these stories. Then he looked at each of the people who listened (*look into the eyes of each child as you say these lines*) and said, "Each of you is far more precious to me than the sheep was to that shepherd, or the coin was to that woman."

Prayer

■ Dear God, we thank you that we are more precious to you than the sheep was to the shepherd or the coin was to the woman. *Amen.*

Thank the children for joining you and invite them to return to their seats.

Luke 15:11-32

"He ran, threw his arms around his son, and kissed him." (Luke 15:20b, _Today's English Version_)

Summary

In this reading from the Gospel of Luke, Jesus illustrates the depth of God's love with the parable of the lost son. In today's homily, children hear the story, then learn that they too, like the lost son, are special children beloved by God.

Materials

Bible
sheet or blanket

Homily

Invite the children to come forward for today's homily. Ask them to sit in a semicircle around you.

Hold the Bible open to the Gospel of Luke as you tell today's story:

Jesus told a story. "Once there was a man who had two sons. He loved both of his sons very much.

"One day the younger of the two sons said to his father, 'Dad, I'm tired of life here in the country. I'm tired of working for you. I'm tired of seeing the same hills and trees and people day after day. Let me have my share of the family money. I'm leaving to see the world.'

"The father felt sad that his son wanted to leave, but he knew that at some point children need to make their own choices and travel their own path, so he gave his son what he asked.

"The father sighed as his son disappeared over the hill.

"The son traveled far away. He saw new places and met interesting people. Best of all, he made all his own choices.

"But not all his choices were good ones. He spent his money —_all_ his money—without ever finding a good job or a place to live. He grew very hungry. He took a job feeding pigs, but even that didn't pay him enough to eat. The boy felt lonely and lost.

"One day, as he sat feeding the pigs, feeling so hungry that even what the pigs were eating began to look tasty, he asked out loud, 'Oh, why did I ever leave home?' Not a pig answered.

"And then he asked, 'Would my father take me back home?' And again the pigs didn't answer.

"And finally he asked, 'Would he take me back if I admit I was wrong and ask him to forgive me?' And this time, one little piglet, watching him from off in a corner, said, 'Oink.'

"So the son headed home.

"When he was still a long way from home, tired from walking and wondering if his father would even talk to him, he looked and saw—*his father!* His father was running up the road toward him.

"The boy stopped. He waited, afraid. Would his father shoo him away? demand his money back? yell at him for his bad choices?

"The father kept running, and, out of breath and smiling from ear to ear, threw his arms around his son. 'Oh, my son,' he said, 'my special child. You have come home.'

"The boy thought his ribs might crack, his father hugged him so hard. The father cried. The boy cried.

"And they walked the rest of the way home, arms around each other."

With the children, discuss:
- Who was lost in today's story?
- Who was waiting in today's story? For what was he waiting?
- What does the father do when he sees his lost son coming home?
- Jesus told this story to tell us something about God, our heavenly Father. How is God like the father in our story?

Invite one child to come forward and crouch on the floor. Ask four children to each take a corner of a sheet or blanket and to cover the crouching child. Say:
- Where's God's special child, *(name of child under sheet)*?
- Is he (or she) in my pocket? *(Let other children answer No.)*
- Is he (or she) out in the hall? *(No.)*
- Is he or she under a chair? *(No.)*

After several silly questions, ask again:
- Where *is* God's special child, *(name)*?

At this point ask the children holding the blanket to lift it high, revealing the hidden child. All children shout:
- Here's God's special child, *(name)!*

Invite children to hug the child as he or she returns to the group, then repeat the game giving all children who wish to take part a chance to be lost, found and welcomed back.

Conclude the homily by asking:
- How does it feel to be lost?
- How does it feel to be found?
- How does it feel to be welcomed back and hugged?
- How does it feel to know that we are God's special children?

Prayer

- God, thanks for always finding us, always loving us, always holding us close to you. *Amen.*

Thank the children for joining you and invite them to return to their seats.

74

Luke 16:1-13

"No servant can be a slave of two masters; such a slave will hate one and love the other or will be loyal to one and despise the other. You cannot serve both God and money."
(Luke 16:13, *Today's English Version*)

Summary

In this reading from the Gospel of Luke, Jesus tells the parable of the shrewd manager. In today's homily, children are first challenged to think about their individual responses to money, then listen to Jesus' parable.

Materials

Bible
50-100 pennies
collection basket or plate typically used in your parish

Homily

Invite the children to come forward for today's homily. Ask them to stand in a circle around you, facing outward. Invite the children to close their eyes tight.

When children have turned away, scatter the pennies over the floor in the center of the circle.

Invite the children to open their eyes and turn around. Let them react to the pennies; some may pick up coins to put in their pockets; others may ask questions. Let

children act and react as they will.

After about 30 seconds, ask:
- How did you feel when you turned around and saw all the pennies? What did you think?
- How do we feel when we find money?
- What do we like about money?
- What *don't* we like about money?
- What shall we do with the money we found?

As you reflect, be careful not to dictate the children's responses, nor to let the majority of the children dictate to the minority. Some children may volunteer a "religious" answer, such as offering the coins to the Church.

Encourage these children in their responses, while protecting the right of another child to take his or her pennies home. The value of the experience lies in the challenge to each child to consider his or her feelings in relationship to money.

Explain:
- In today's gospel, Jesus talks about money, and that's the story I want to tell you today.

Hold the Bible open to the Gospel of Luke as you tell today's story:

The friends of Jesus were talking. They said, "It's hard to follow you, Jesus. We've got no place to sleep. We never know what we'll get to eat. We want homes and money and food, like everyone else."

So Jesus turned to them and said, "I'll tell you a story.

"I'll tell you about a man who stole and cheated his master. His master found out, and got *angry*. 'Finish up your work,' the master said, 'then get out, you good-for-nothing servant!'

"The man was scared, through and through. 'What will happen to me,' he moaned. 'I can't dig. I can't beg. I don't want to starve in the street.'

"And that man got smart," said Jesus. "That man gave up some of that money. He gave it back to people he had cheated, so they would help him now that hard times had come."

Jesus stopped talking. He looked at his disciples and asked, "Who did that man love more? himself or money?"

Then Jesus asked again, "And how about you? Who will you love more, God or money?"

Discuss with the children:
- Jesus says money is not very important, but the choices we make about money *are* important.
- Even our small choices are important to God, because *we* are important to God. God cares about the choices we make.
- What kinds of choices about money do we make at home? at school? with our friends?
- How do you think God feels about the choices we make? Why?

Pass around the basket or plate. Invite each child to hold the basket or plate as he or she makes an offering to God. Explain that this could be a penny, a thank you for a favorite pet or a simple praise of God.

It is likely that some of the children will place one or more of their pennies in the basket.

Prayer

- Dear God, help us to love you more than we love money. Help us to love you more than the things that money can buy. *Amen.*

Thank the children for joining you and invite them to return to their seats.

Luke 16:19-31

"There was once a rich man who dressed in the most expensive clothes and lived in great luxury every day. There was also a poor man named Lazarus..." (Luke 16:19-20a, *Today's English Version*)

Summary

In this reading from the Gospel of Luke, Jesus uses the parable of the rich man to illustrate the importance of helping the poor. In today's homily, children describe what they would do with $100, then hear today's story and learn a simple song about helping others.

Materials

Bible
$100 bill (either real or from a board game or photocopied from the illustration on page 78)

Invite the children to come forward for today's homily. Ask them to sit in a semicircle around you.

Pass around the real or imitation $100 bill. Explain:
■ Imagine someone gave you this much money: a hundred dollars.
■ What are some things you would do with a hundred dollars? *(Welcome a variety of responses from children.)*

Do not show approval or disapproval of children's choices; for example, avoid saying, "I don't think guns are a nice thing to buy."

Do not correct their misunderstandings about prices; for example, do not say, "You can't get a swimming pool for one hundred dollars."

End the activity by saying:
■ Jesus once told a story about a man who was so rich, he could have anything he wanted—and that's the story I'm going to tell you today.

Hold the Bible open to the Gospel of Luke as you tell today's story:

Once there was a very rich man. "I want to own everything," he said.

He said to his servants, "Bring me clothes to wear." And his servants brought him new clothes to wear. But the rich man wanted more.

He said to his servants, "Bring me plenty of food to eat." And his servants brought him good food to eat. But the rich man wanted more.

He said to his servants, "Bring me too much food to eat." And his servants brought him too much food to eat. The rich man ate and ate, dropping food right on the floor.

Nearby lived a poor, hungry man named Lazarus. He didn't have a home. He didn't have new clothes. He didn't have good food to eat. "I'm hungry," said Lazarus.

He went to the rich man and said, "Can I have clothes?"

"No," said the rich man.

"Can I have food?" asked Lazarus.

"No," said the rich man.

"Can I at least have the food that dropped on the floor?" asked Lazarus.

"No," said the rich man.

So Lazarus was still hungry.

One day the rich man died. God said to him, "I'm not happy with you. You should have given Lazarus some of your food to eat. You should have given him clothes to wear. I wanted you to do good things for other people. That would have made me happy!"

When Lazarus died, the angels carried him to heaven to feast on tasty foods forever.

If time allows, teach the children to sing the words below to the tune of "The More We Get Together." (This is the same tune as "Did You Ever See a Lassie?") When you teach the song, use the word *we* rather than *names* in the places marked with italics.

> The more that we help others,
> Help others, help others,
> The more that we help others,
> The happier God is.
> For (*name*) can help others,
> And (*name*) can help others,
> The more that we help others,
> The happier God is.

Prayer

■ God, thank you for the people who help us every day. Help us to help others, too. *Amen.*

Thank the children for joining you and invite them to return to their seats.

Luke 17:5-10

The Lord answered, "If you had faith as big as a mustard seed, you could say to this mulberry tree, 'Pull yourself up by the roots and plant yourself in the sea!' and it would obey you." (Luke 17:6, *Today's English Version*)

Summary

In this reading from the Gospel of Luke, Jesus uses the illustration of the tiny mustard seed to teach the power of even a small amount of faith. In today's homily, children hear this story, then learn the words and motions to a simple action rhyme.

Materials

Bible
mustard seeds

Homily

Invite the children to come forward for today's homily. Ask them to sit in a semicircle around you.

Hold the Bible open to the Gospel of Luke as you tell today's story:

Jesus was God's servant.

Jesus came to serve the sick. He held them and healed them.

Jesus came to serve people who wanted to know more about

God. Jesus told them stories about God.

Jesus came to serve the hungry. He gave bread and fish to the hungry.

One day Jesus and his friends rested under the leafy branches of a large tree, a mulberry tree. The friends of Jesus said, "We want to do what you can do! Make our faith in God grow!"

Jesus said, "I'm glad you want to do what I do! I'm glad you want your faith in God to grow!"

Jesus held a tiny mustard seed in his hand. (*Show children a mustard seed, cradled in the palm of your hand.*) He said, "If

you have as much faith as this, you could even make this big tree jump in the sea! But even better, you could serve others, just as I do. Pray for more faith!"

Let children pass the mustard seed from palm to palm around the circle. You might softly repeat the last few sentences of the story as the children pass the seed.

If you wish, discuss with the children:
■ Jesus said that faith helps us serve others.
■ How does our faith help us to serve others?

Teach the children the words and motions to this action rhyme:

Faith as small as a mustard seed,
(Hold right hand out, palm up. Point left index finger into palm.)

can make a mighty, mighty tree,
(Stretch fingers wide; spread hands up and out to make a leafy "tree.")

jump into the deep blue sea!
(Keep fingers and hands stretched as you take a big jump forward.)

Prayer

■ God, thanks for giving us faith. Give us even more faith. *Amen.*

Thank the children for joining you and invite them to return to their seats.

Luke 17:11-19

Jesus spoke up, "There were ten who were healed; where are the other nine? Why is this foreigner the only one who came back to give thanks to God?" (Luke 17:17-18;
*Today's English Version***)**

Summary

In this reading from the Gospel of Luke, Jesus heals ten men who suffer from a skin disease, but only one returns to thank him. In today's homily, children hear this story, then thank God for the blessings of the last week.

Materials

Bible
small basket
dozens of small, natural objects, for
   example, shells, wood chips,
   pine cones, stones, etc.

Homily

Invite the children to come forward for today's homily. Ask them to sit in a semicircle around you.

Hold the Bible open to the Gospel of Luke as you tell today's story:

One day Jesus and his friends were on the road between Samaria and Galilee. Suddenly, far off in the distance, they saw ten men.

"They have skin disease," said one friend.

"We must stay far away from them," said another friend, "or we might catch it, too."

But the ten men had seen Jesus, and they were calling to him. "Jesus! Master! Save us! Have pity on us!"

Jesus walked right up to the men. He said to them, "Go. Show yourselves to the priests."

Jesus' friends looked at one another. Go to the priests? People who were healed were supposed to show themselves to the priests. Were the ten men already healed?

The ten men walked away down the road. As they walked, they looked down at their skin. "My skin is clean," said one.

"So is mine," said another.

"We're healed!" whispered a third. "Jesus healed us!"

All the men began to talk at once, as they walked faster and faster down the road. But one of the men turned and threw his arms up into the sky.

"Thank God, I'm healed," he yelled. And he called out praises to God as he ran back down the road to Jesus.

When the man reached Jesus, he threw himself down on the ground. "Thank you, Jesus! Thank you for healing me!"

Jesus looked at the man with love and then looked at his friends. "Weren't ten men healed?" asked Jesus. "Where are the other nine?"

Then Jesus helped the man to his feet. "Go on your way," said Jesus. "Your faith has made you well."

Place the basket in the center of the semicircle of children. Around the basket scatter the natural materials (pinecones, shells, wood chips, etc.).

Explain:
- Each of us enjoyed many good things during this past week: food that we ate, clothes that we wore, friends or families that cared for us.
- For each good thing that you can name, you can put one object in the basket.
- Let's see if, together, we can make this basket overflow.

Help children give specific thanks ("oatmeal cookies" and "my favorite jeans" rather than "food" and "clothing") as they fill the basket.

When the basket is as filled or overflowing as possible, ask:
- How many men were healed in today's story about Jesus?
- How many men came back to thank Jesus?
- When can we remember to say thank you to God for all the good things we named in our thank-you basket?

Prayer
- Dear God, thank you for all the good gifts you give us, every day. *Amen.*

Thank the children for joining you and invite them to return to their seats.

Luke 18:1-8a

"Now, will God not judge in favor of his own people who cry to him day and night for help? Will he be slow to help them? I tell you, he will judge in their favor and do it quickly." (Luke 18:7-8a, *Today's English Version***)**

Summary

In this reading from the Gospel of Luke, Jesus illustrates God's responsiveness to our prayers with the parable of the widow and the judge. In today's homily, children first illustrate the difference between wants and needs, then hear and discuss the story.

Materials

Bible
2 sheets of poster board, one titled *Needs* and the other titled *Wants*
colored felt markers
easels or stands to hold the posters upright

Homily

Invite the children to come forward for today's homily. Ask them to sit in a semicircle around you.

Show children the two posters. With the children, discuss:
■ What is a *need*? What things do we need every day?

Invite several children to draw on the *Need* poster pictures of things they believe we need every day.

Continue:
■ What is a *want*? What things do we want?

Invite several children to draw on the *Want* poster pictures of things they want.

Continue:
■ Is what we *need* always the same as what we *want*?
■ Do we all need the same things?
■ How do we get things that we need?
■ Once Jesus told a story about a woman who had trouble getting what she needed; that's the story I'm going to tell you today.

Hold the Bible open to the Gospel of Luke as you tell today's story:

Once there was a judge who was not just or fair at all. If people came and said, "You must help us, judge," the judge would say, "Hah! Who cares about you?"

And if the people said, "But you're supposed to help us!

That's God's law," the judge would say, "Hah! Who cares about God?"

One day a woman came to the judge and said, "You must help me, judge. I am a widow. My husband has died, and I have an enemy who is taking my money."

But the judge said, "Hah! Who cares about you?"

But the widow came back the very next day and said, "I'm not giving up, judge! I have an enemy who is cheating me out of my money—and it's *your* job to help me."

The judge said, "Hah! I'll never help you, so you might as well give up right now."

But the widow did not give up. She came back day after day, saying, "Do your job, judge! Protect me against my enemy!"

The unfair judge tried to get rid of her every way he could think of. He yelled at her one day. He ignored her the next day. He made fun of her the day after

that and called her names the day after that.

But every day the widow came back. Finally, the unfair judge said, "I give up! If I don't give this woman what she needs, she'll never stop pestering me." And he said to the widow, "You win! I'll do my job!" And he did.

Discuss with the children:
■ Why do you think Jesus told this story?
■ What does the Bible say about why Jesus told this story? (*Read Luke 18:1 aloud.*)
■ Jesus tells us that we can pray to God over and over again, just as the widow went to the judge over and over.
■ But God is different from the judge; God *wants* to answer us. God wants to "judge in our favor." That means God wants to make decisions that are right for us.

Prayer

■ Thank you, God, for hearing us right away when we pray. *Amen.*

Thank the children for joining you and invite them to return to their seats.

Luke 18:9-14

"I tell you," said Jesus, "the tax collector, and not the Pharisee, was in the right with God when he went home. For those who make themselves great will be humbled, and those who humble themselves will be made great." (Luke 18:14, *Today's English Version***)**

Summary

In this reading from the Gospel of Luke, Jesus encourages humility through the parable of the Pharisee and the tax collector. In today's homily, children first discuss forgiveness, hear the story and experience God's forgiveness by "throwing away" something they feel sorry for.

Materials

Bible
slips of paper
pencils
glue sticks
metal wastebasket
optional:
matches
water

Homily

Invite the children to come forward for today's homily. Ask them to sit in a semicircle around you.

With the children, discuss:

■ What does it mean to forgive?
■ How does it feel when you forgive someone?
■ When do we need people to forgive us?
■ How does it feel when someone forgives you?
■ Sometimes in church we ask God to forgive us.
■ When do we need God to forgive us?
■ God always hears our prayers. God forgives us right away when we are sorry.
■ How does it feel to know God is ready to forgive us right away?
■ Jesus once told a story about forgiveness, and that's the story I want to tell you today.

Hold the Bible open to the Gospel of Luke as you tell today's story:

Once, two men went up to the temple to pray. The first man was a Pharisee who tried very hard to keep God's law. The second man was a tax collector, who had cheated many people out of their money.

The Pharisee stood up, spread out his arms, and prayed, "God, thank you that I am not like everyone else. Thank you that I keep your law so well. I'm not greedy, like that tax collector over there. I don't cheat people. I don't lie to you or to my wife."

The Pharisee felt happier and happier as he thought of what a good man he was. He prayed again, "Two days a week I go without food to show how much I love you, Lord. And I give a tenth of all my money to the temple."

Now the tax collector was praying, too, but he did not feel happy. He did not dare raise up his eyes. He could only look at the ground. He even hit himself on the chest again and again, wishing he could drive out his sadness.

"Lord," the tax collector said—and he could barely hear his own voice—"Lord, I am a sinner. Have mercy on me. Lord, I have done wrong. Forgive me." And this is all he could pray, again and again.

Jesus told this story to his disciples. Then he looked at them and said, "The tax collector went home right with God—and the Pharisee did not."

Prayer

Give each child a slip of paper and a pencil. Explain:

- Think of something you have done that you feel sorry about. You don't have to tell anyone what you are thinking.
- Write or draw what you have done on the slip of paper. No one else will see what you write or draw.
- Fold the paper and glue it closed. *(Show this process to the children.)*

Collect the glued papers in the metal wastebasket. Tell the children that God already forgives what they have done; God throws it away and forgets it forever. If possible, light a match and burn the papers in the basket.

Then ask the children what each one of them would like to say to God this morning. Give time for each child's response, then close with your own spontaneous prayer—perhaps no more than a simple:

- Thank you, God, that you always forgive us when we are sorry. *Amen.*

Thank the children for joining you and invite them to return to their seats.

Luke 19:1-10

**When Jesus came to that place, he
looked up and said to Zacchaeus,
"Hurry down, Zacchaeus, because I
must stay in your house today."**
(Luke 19:5, *Today's English Version*)

Summary

In this reading from the Gospel
of Luke, Jesus invites himself to the
home of Zacchaeus, a despised tax
collector. In today's homily, children first imagine how they might
see Jesus if he were talking to a
thick crowd of people, then hear
and discuss today's story.

Materials

Bible

Homily

Invite the children to come forward for today's homily. Ask them
to sit in a semicircle around you.

Invite the children to imagine seeing Jesus in all kinds of places:
- Imagine Jesus is standing way at
  the back of the church. How
  will we see Jesus?
- Imagine Jesus is at the top of the
  tallest building in town. How
  will we see Jesus?
- Imagine Jesus is in the middle of
  a forest. How will we see Jesus?
- Imagine Jesus is at the bottom of
  a tall, tall cliff—and we are at
  the top. How will we see Jesus?
- Imagine Jesus is standing in the

middle of a crowd of people,
and they are all taller than we
are. How will we see Jesus?

You will probably get some far-
fetched answers! Enjoy the children's abilities to imagine and
create a variety of solutions.

Feel free to omit one or more of
the questions if time is limited,
but be sure to end with the last
question.

Close by saying:
- A man named Zacchaeus had
  that problem once—and this is
  what he did.

Hold the Bible open to the Gospel
of Luke as you tell today's story:

**In Jericho there lived a man
called Zacchaeus. Now Zacchaeus was a small man, but
with big pockets: he was the
richest man in town. Zacchaeus
was a tax collector who had
taken money—too much
money—from everyone in
Jericho.**

**One day Zacchaeus heard a
woman call out, "It's Jesus! He's
walking through Jericho!"**

"Jesus is coming!" thought Zacchaeus. "I must see him."

So Zacchaeus ran to the road, but when he got there, the road was already filled with people. They were crowding and struggling to get a look at Jesus.

Zacchaeus tried to look between people's shoulders, but he couldn't see Jesus. He tried to look between people's legs, but he couldn't see Jesus. He stood on his tiptoes, but he couldn't see Jesus.

Then he turned around and there, by the side of the road, was a sycamore tree. Up went Zacchaeus, hand over hand, branch over branch. He peered through the thick, green leaves and—there! There was Jesus.

And Jesus was looking right at him! "Zacchaeus," called Jesus, with a smile. "Hurry down from there—I'm coming to your house today!"

But then Zacchaeus heard someone in the crowd grumble, "Why is Jesus eating with that man? That man takes our money! That man is nothing but a sinner."

Zacchaeus stood up as tall as he could. "Jesus," he said. "I'm going to give half of my money away to the poor. And if I have cheated anyone, I'll give back four times as much money to that person."

Then Jesus laughed for joy and said, "Today you are no sinner, Zacchaeus! Today you, too, are one of God's own people."

Ask the children to imagine that Jesus is coming to their home for dinner today. Ask:
- How do we feel, knowing that Jesus is coming for dinner?
- What would we give Jesus for dinner?
- What would we say to Jesus?
- What would we do with Jesus?
- What would we like to ask Jesus?

Prayer

- Thank you, God, for sending Jesus to be with us. Help us to welcome him with open arms, as Zacchaeus did. *Amen.*

Thank the children for joining you and invite them to return to their seats.

Luke 19:29-40

"God bless the king who comes in the name of the Lord! Peace in heaven and glory to God!" (Luke 19:38, *Today's English Version*)

Summary

In this reading from the Gospel of Luke, Jesus rides triumphantly into Jerusalem, receiving the praise of the people. In today's homily, children hear this story, then lead parishioners in a joyful chant to Jesus.

Materials

Bible

Homily

Invite the children to come forward for today's homily. Ask them to sit in a semicircle around you.

Hold the Bible open to the Gospel of Luke as you tell today's story:

"It's time to head to the city, Jerusalem," Jesus said to his disciples. It was a perfect day. Sunshine flooded around them. A breeze brought the scent of freshly blooming flowers. A few white clouds floated through the blue sky.

As they were walking, Jesus said to two of his friends, "See that village up ahead? There's a colt tied up there. It's never been ridden. Get it for me and bring it here while we wait and rest awhile."

Jesus' friends looked at each other. "But Jesus," said one, "isn't that, like, stealing?"

"It will be okay," Jesus said. "Just tell the owner, 'The Master needs it.'"

So the two friends of Jesus went ahead. And sure enough, there was a colt, never ridden, tied up in the village. "This is weird," said the one friend, as he untied the colt.

"Hey, what are you doing?" a woman asked. Jesus' friends jumped. "That's *my* colt," another woman said.

"Um...the Master needs this colt?" said one of them, hesitantly.

"Ah, the Master has need of it. Take it then," said the woman.

The friends returned with the colt. Jesus climbed on and they continued toward Jerusalem.

As they drew closer to the city, a strange and wonderful thing happened. People started gathering around Jesus, people who had heard him preach, people who had been healed, friends and families of people Jesus' had helped. They said wonderful things about Jesus. They threw their coats down in front of Jesus and the colt. They reached out to touch him. They thanked him.

The crowd grew. More and more people joined them. On one side of the road they shouted, "God bless the king who comes in the name of the Lord!" *(Invite the children to repeat this in unison with you several times.)*

The other side of the road answered, "Peace in heaven and glory to God!" *(Invite the children to repeat this in unison with you several times.)*

Someone in the crowd—someone who didn't like Jesus much—pushed his way forward and said to Jesus, "Hey, tell these people to quiet down!"

Jesus laughed. "I can't! If I did, then even the stones along the road would shout instead!"

And on went the joyful, shouting crowd, with Jesus in the middle, all the way into Jerusalem.

Invite the children—and all parishioners—to join you in joyfully echoing the shouts of the people on the road to Jerusalem. Ask half the children to stand to one side of the church, facing the parishioners; place the other half of the children on the other side, also facing the parishioners.

Have half of the children lead the parishioners seated on their side in calling out in unison:
■ God bless the king who comes in the name of the Lord!

The other half of the children then lead the parishioners seated on their side in responding in unison with:
■ Peace in heaven and glory to God!

Encourage both children and parishioners to shout loudly! Repeat the joyful shout and response a number of times before inviting the children to return to their seats.

Prayer
■ All praise to you, King Jesus! *Amen.*

Luke 20:27-38

"They will be like angels and cannot die. They are the children of God, because they have risen from death."
(Luke 20:36, *Today's English Version*)

Summary

In this reading from the Gospel of Luke, Jesus answers the Sadducees' riddle about life after death. In today's homily, children first share riddles, then hear today's story.

Materials

Bible
a paper bag in which you have hidden:
> an apple cut in half
> a coin
> a pea

Homily

Invite the children to come forward for today's homily. Ask them to sit in a semicircle around you.

Hold up half the apple and say:
■ I have a riddle for you. What looks like half an apple?

After children have guessed, show the other half of the apple and say:
■ The other half of the apple.

Continue:
■ What has a head and a tail but no body? *(Show the coin and say, "a coin.")*
■ Which letter of the alphabet grows in the garden? *(Show the pea and say, "a pea.")*

■ When do children have four feet? *(Invite two children to stand together in the center of the semicircle. Say, "When there are two of them.")*

Ask the children if they know any riddles. (You may want to define a riddle as a tricky question.) End the activity by saying:
■ Once some people asked Jesus a riddle—a tricky question—and that's the story I'm going to tell you today.

Hold the Bible open to the Gospel of Luke as you tell today's story:

One day Jesus was teaching. "When we die," said Jesus, "God will give us new life. We will live with God and never die again."

Some people who heard Jesus did not believe him.

"New life!" said one of them. "That's silly."

"When you're dead, you're dead," said another. "There's no such thing as new life."

"I have an idea," said a third. "We'll make up a riddle for Jesus. We'll show him how silly this teaching about new life is."

So the people who did not believe came to Jesus. "Teacher," they said, "we have a riddle for you.

"Once there was a woman who married a man. But the man died, so the woman married his brother. This man died, too, so the woman married the third brother.

"The third brother died and the woman married the fourth brother. The fifth brother, the sixth brother and the seventh brother—the woman married each one, and each one died.

"After some time, the woman died, too. Now this is the riddle: when the woman and the seven brothers rise to new life, which brother will be her husband?"

But Jesus just shook his head. "New life isn't like your riddle. When God gives people new life, they don't marry. And they never die again. The woman and each brother will not be husband and wife anymore, but they will live forever."

"I still don't believe that," said one person.

But another person looked at Jesus and thought about what he had said. Was Jesus right? Could God really give new life that never ends?

Allow children to answer these final questions, if they wish.

Prayer

◼ Dear God, thank you for Jesus who brings us to new life. May we live forever with you and all who love you in the land of light and joy. *Amen.*

Thank the children for joining you and invite them to return to their seats.

Luke 21:5-19

"But not a single hair from your heads will be lost. Stand firm, and you will save yourselves." (Luke 21:18-19, *Today's English Version*)

Summary

In this reading from the Gospel of Luke, Jesus speaks of coming persecution and disaster, concluding with a promise of salvation. In today's homily, children talk about hard times, hear today's story and receive assurance of God's constant love and presence.

Materials

Bible
pennies or nickels, one per child

Homily

Invite the children to come forward for today's homily. Ask them to sit in a semicircle around you.

Give each child a coin. Ask an older child to read aloud what is printed on the coin: *In God we trust.* Ask:

- What does it mean to trust in God?
- When is it hardest to trust in God?
- Why is trusting in God harder during hard times?
- What hard times have we had lately at home? at school? with friends?
- Jesus once talked about hard times, and that's the story I want to tell you today.

Hold the Bible open to the Gospel of Luke as you tell today's story. As indicated in the story, have children respond with the phrase written on their coins: *In God we trust.*

"Tough times are coming," Jesus said to his friends.

They all stopped talking. "What did you say?" someone asked. "Did you say 'tough times'?" No one wanted to hear about tough times. They only wanted good times, happy times, joyful times.

"Yes," said Jesus. "That's what I said. Tough times are coming. I wish it were not so, but it is."

"What kind of tough times, Jesus?"

Jesus continued: "Times when people will be mean to you."

"What shall we do when people are mean to us?"

"Trust in God," Jesus said. *(Invite the children to say in unison, "In God we trust.")*

Jesus continued: "There will be times when people call you names."

"What shall we do when people call us names?"

"Trust in God," Jesus said. *(Children say in unison, "In God we trust.")*

Jesus continued: "There will be times when people accuse you of things you have not done."

"What shall we do when people accuse us of things we have not done?"

"Trust in God," Jesus said. *(Children say in unison, "In God we trust.")*

Jesus said, "Yes, even my friends can expect to have hard times. We will have hard times all our lives, all of us. But God is always with us through all the hard times. Always. Always."

(Children respond one final time with, "In God we trust.")

Prayer

■ God, we don't like hard times, but we are very glad you are always with us in hard times. *Amen.*

Thank the children for joining you and invite them to return to their seats.

Luke 21:15-28

"Then the Son of Man will appear, coming in a cloud with great power and glory." (Luke 21:27, _Today's English Version_)

Summary

In this reading from the Gospel of Luke, Jesus speaks of his second coming. In today's homily, children hear today's story, then learn a song about Jesus' second coming and use the song in a game that welcomes Jesus.

Materials

Bible

Homily

Invite the children to come forward for today's homily. Ask them to sit in a semicircle around you.

Begin the homily by teaching children this response:

> _Homilist:_ Who's coming?

> _Children:_ Jesus is coming.

To help them learn the response, encourage children to vary their response by whispering, singing, speaking high or low, etc. Explain to the children that they can help tell today's homily by calling out the answer whenever they hear the question.

Hold the Bible open to the Gospel of Luke as you tell today's story:

Who's coming?

Jesus is coming!

Jesus says, "Listen, my friends! I love you! I will come to you again some day so that you can see me and touch me and hug me, too."

Who's coming?

Jesus is coming!

Jesus says, "Listen, my friends! One day strange things will happen in the sky. The sun and the moon will run around because I'm coming to be with you, my friends!"

Who's coming?

Jesus is coming!

Jesus says, "Listen, my friends! One day you will look up in the sky and you will see me, coming to be with you! Hooray! I will come and be with you forever, my friends!"

Who's coming?

Jesus is coming!

(*Encourage children to clap and cheer for Jesus.*)

Teach children to sing this song to the tune of "Frere Jacques":

> Who is coming? Who is coming?
> Jesus Christ! Jesus Christ!
> Jesus Christ is coming.
> Jesus Christ is coming.
> Jesus Christ. Jesus Christ.

Ask for a volunteer to be the first *Jesus. Jesus* crouches down, hiding his or her head. Invite the other children to join hands with you and form a circle around *Jesus.*

Walk with the children in a circle around *Jesus* as you sing the song together. When the last *Jesus Christ* is sung, *Jesus* jumps up and stands tall. The children drop hands and run to welcome *Jesus.*

Repeat with other volunteers playing the role of *Jesus.*

Prayer

■ Jesus, we welcome you. *Amen.*

Thank the children for joining you and invite them to return to their seats. You might invite the parishioners to sing "Who Is Coming?" as children return, welcoming the children with hugs once they find their seats.

96

Luke (19:28-40)
22:39–24:10

"Remember what he said to you while he was in Galilee: 'The Son of Man must be handed over to the sinners, be crucified, and three days later rise to life.'" (Luke 24:6b-7, *Today's English Version*)

Summary

In this reading from the Gospel of Luke, Jesus rides into Jerusalem, eats a final meal with his disciples, is arrested, tried and crucified. He rises to new life. In today's homily, children discuss several symbols related to Holy Week and Easter, then hear today's story.

Note: If you wish, you may omit Jesus' triumphal entry into Jerusalem from this homily. Skip the discussion of the palm branch and start the story at the asterisk.

Materials

Bible
palm branch
bread and wine (or grape juice)
cross
colored Easter egg or photo or
    drawing of a butterfly

Homily

Invite the children to come forward for today's homily. Ask them to sit in a semicircle around you.

Show children the palm branch. Ask:
■ When do we see palm branches like this used in church?
■ What do you think of when you see the palm branch?

Show children the bread and wine. Ask:
■ When do we see bread and wine like this used in church?
■ What do you think of when you see the bread and wine?

Show children the cross. Ask:
■ When do we see a cross like this used in church?
■ What do you think of when you see a cross?

Show children the Easter egg or butterfly. Ask:
■ When do we see a butterfly (or Easter egg) like this?
■ What do you think of when you see a butterfly (Easter egg)?

If children have difficulty answering any of these questions, encourage them to listen for the answers in today's story.

Hold the Bible open to the Gospel of Luke as you tell today's story.

"Go to the village," Jesus told his friends, "and find a colt for me." So the friends went and found the animal. They spread their robes over the colt and helped Jesus climb on.

Then Jesus rode into Jerusalem. People ran to see him. They pulled branches from palm trees and waved the long leaves at Jesus, shouting, "God bless our king! God bless King Jesus!"

(Hold up the palm branch.) And that is why we sometimes see palm branches in church. We wave palms and sing, "God bless our King."

*Jesus knew that people were planning to kill him. He sat with his friends to eat a last meal together. "Eat this bread," said Jesus, "and drink this wine until I come again."

(Hold up the bread and wine.) And that is why we share bread and wine in church. We remember Jesus' death. We pray for him to come again.

Soldiers came to arrest Jesus. They nailed him to a wooden cross, and there Jesus died.

(Hold up the cross.) And that is why we honor the cross of Jesus in our church. On that cross, Jesus gave his love to the whole world.

Jesus' friends put his dead body into a cave and rolled a huge stone over the door. They cried. "We will never see Jesus again," they said.

Friday evening the sun set. Saturday evening the sun set.

Early on Sunday morning several women who were friends of Jesus went to visit the cave. The stone was rolled away! Jesus wasn't there!

Two men in bright, shining clothes stood beside the women and said, "Why are you looking here among the dead for someone who is alive? Jesus is not here. He is risen! He is alive!"

So the women ran to tell the amazing news that first Easter morning.

(Hold up the Easter egg or butterfly.) And that is why we celebrate Easter. We tell our families, our friends, our world the amazing news: Jesus is risen! Jesus is alive!

Prayer

■ Dear God, thank you for sending Jesus to us and to all people. Thank you for giving Jesus new life. *Amen.*

Thank the children for joining you and invite them to return to their seats.

Luke 23:35-43

**Above him were written these
words: "This is the King of the Jews!"
(Luke 23:38, *Today's English Version*)**

Summary

In this reading from the Gospel of Luke, Jesus hangs on the cross, enduring ridicule as the "king of the Jews." In today's homily, children talk about kings, hear today's story and learn a simple song that identifies Jesus as their King.

Materials

Bible
paper crown (see **note** below)
accompanist for the song "Our King," printed on page 32

Note: Before the homily, form a crown 15" high by making a circle with a 15" x 36" paper strip or cutting out the bottom of a round, gallon ice cream carton. (Cover a carton crown with construction paper.) Cut large notches in the paper strip or the carton to create the points of the crown. You might want to decorate the crown with bits of construction paper, ribbon, etc. Cut out page 32 for the accompanist.

Homily

Invite the children to come forward for today's homily. Ask them to sit in a semicircle around you.

Show children the crown created **before the homily**. Discuss:

- Can you tell me what this is?
- That's right, it's a crown. Who wears a crown?
- In some fairy tales we know, there are kings and queens. In some countries today, there are kings and queens. And kings and queens wear crowns.
- What do queens and kings do?
- That's right, queens and kings rule. They are the bosses of everything in the lands where they live and rule. People have to do what queens and kings tell them to do.
- Jesus is called *King*, too. Today's story is about our King, Jesus.

Hold the Bible open to the Gospel of Luke as you tell today's story. Today's story employs a rhythmic refrain: *Jesus is our King*. As you tell the story, pause before each repetition of the refrain, signaling with your eyes and face that children can join in:

Jesus is our King. Jesus came to bring people into God's kingdom.

Jesus is our King.

Jesus healed people so that they could be well in God's kingdom.

Jesus is our King.

Jesus taught people so that they could know the joy of God's kingdom.

99

Jesus is our King.

Jesus raised people from the dead so that they could live forever in God's kingdom.

Jesus is our King.

But some people were angry at Jesus. They killed Jesus: they nailed Jesus, our King, to a cross.

At the cross, some people made fun of Jesus, our King. "If you are a King," they said, "Come down from there. If you can save others, save yourself!"

Two prisoners were nailed to crosses that day, one on each side of Jesus, our King. One of them made fun of Jesus, too.

But the other said, "Jesus, you are my King, even here on the cross. Jesus, remember me in God's kingdom."

And Jesus said, "Today, I tell you, you will be with me as we wait for God's new life together."

Even on the cross, Jesus brought this prisoner into God's kingdom.

Jesus is our King.

There on the cross, Jesus died. They sealed him in a tomb, Jesus, our King.

But on the third day, Jesus rose. God gave Jesus new life that would never end.

Jesus is our King.

Forever, Jesus will bring people into God's kingdom.

Forever, Jesus will heal people to be whole in God's kingdom.

Forever, Jesus will teach people to know the joy of God's kingdom.

Forever: *Jesus is our King.*

Lead children (and the parishioners) in singing "Our King," printed on page 32. The tune is the traditional "Do Lord."

Prayer

■ Thank you, King Jesus, for new life, for healing, for joy. Thank you, King Jesus. *Amen.*

Thank the children for joining you and invite them to return to their seats.

Luke 24:13-35

**They said to each other,
"Wasn't it like a fire burning in
us when he talked to us on
the road and explained the
Scriptures to us?" (Luke 24:32,
Today's English Version)**

Summary

In this reading from the Gospel of Luke, the resurrected Jesus walks and talks with two friends on the road to Emmaus. In today's homily, children talk about their friendships, hear today's story and discuss concrete ways in which they can be friends with Jesus today.

Materials

Bible

Homily

Invite the children to come forward for today's homily. Ask them to sit in a semicircle around you.

Begin the homily by inviting children to tell you what happened after Jesus' death. Simple questions, such as "What happened next?" or "Did Jesus stay dead?" help elicit children's answers. Be certain that children have included an account of Jesus' resurrection.

Invite children to think of ways they like to spend time with their friends and family. How do they like to eat? work? play? travel?

Say:
■ Today's story tells about how two people spent time with a very special friend.

Hold the Bible open to the Gospel of Luke as you tell today's story. **Note:** The word *Emmaus* is pronounced Em-MAY-us:

Two friends of Jesus were walking to a town called Emmaus. The two friends were talking together about everything that had happened.

"But Jesus can't be alive!" said one friend. "I saw his body go into the tomb."

"But the women say he is alive," said the other friend. "Why would they say that if Jesus were dead?"

A stranger came up to the two friend and began to walk along with them. "What are you talking about?" he asked. "Who is this Jesus?"

"Are you the only person who doesn't know what has been happening?" exclaimed one friend.

"Everyone knows that our friend Jesus was from God," said the other friend. "But people killed him anyway. That was hard enough to believe— we thought Jesus was too powerful to be killed."

"But now some women in our group have surprised us," said the first friend. "They went to his tomb, but his body was not there. They came back and told us they had seen a vision of angels who said he is alive. We don't know what to think!"

The stranger answered them, "You certainly are slow to understand. The Bible said all this would happen; let me explain it to you."

Then he told them stories from the Bible, and explained how the Bible told all about Jesus, too. The friends loved to listen to the man talk; they loved to hear his stories.

When they got to Emmaus, it was almost dark. "Stay with us," the two friends begged the stranger. "We want to be with you still."

The stranger went inside with the two friends. When they sat down to eat together, he took bread, said the blessing, then broke the bread and gave it to them. All of a sudden they recognized the stranger.

"It's you, Jesus!" they exclaimed, but he vanished from their sight.

"We should have known!" they said. "When he explained all those stories, didn't it sound like the Jesus we love?"

Jumping up, they ran back to Jerusalem to tell all their friends that what the women had said was indeed true. Jesus was alive!

Discuss:
- Who did the two friends meet on the road?
- What did Jesus do with his friends? *(walked together, explained scripture, talked, broke bread, etc.)*
- Do we ever feel as if we are spending time with Jesus? When?
- Jesus still spends time with each of us in many special ways.
- When we share bread and wine in church, we are sharing a special meal with Jesus.
- When we hear God's word from the Bible, we are hearing special words from Jesus.
- When we pray or talk to Jesus, Jesus listens to us.
- When we gather together to think about Jesus or talk about Jesus or just love one another, Jesus says he will be right here with us.

Prayer
- Glory to you, God, for sending Jesus to be our friend and for loving each one of us. *Amen.*

Thank the children for joining you and invite them to return to their seats.

Luke 24:35-48

"Look at my hands and my feet, and see that it is I myself. Feel me, and you will know, for a ghost doesn't have flesh and bones, as you can see I have." (Luke 24:39, *Today's English Version***)**

Summary

In this reading from the Gospel of Luke, Jesus appears to his disciples after his resurrection. In today's homily, children first experiment with touch, then hear this story.

Materials

Bible

a basket or box in which are hidden miscellaneous items with a variety of textures: textured cloth (velvet, burlap, etc.), sandpaper, plastic or vinyl, onion with papery skin, bark, balls of yarn, wet spaghetti, unspun wool, etc.

plate of non-messy finger food—crackers, cheese, fruit, etc.

Homily

Invite the children to come forward for today's homily. Ask them to sit in a semicircle around you.

Bring out the basket or box of items. Invite a volunteer to close his or her eyes. (You can offer a blindfold, but let the child choose whether to wear it. Many young children dislike blindfolds.)

Ask the volunteer to pick one item from the basket or box. Encourage the volunteer to touch the item in many ways; for example, children can rub a ball of yarn against a cheek or stroke it with their fingers.

Ask the other children not to name the item being handled. The volunteer need not guess the name of the object, but can simply explore it any way he or she chooses. Invite other volunteers, one at a time, to explore new items.

Close by saying:
- We can touch and feel many things.
- Someone special in today's story says, "Touch me!" Listen and find out who.

Hold the Bible open to the Gospel of Luke as you tell today's story:

Jesus' friends feel sad because Jesus is no longer with them.

Suddenly Jesus is with them! *(Encourage children to greet Jesus.)*

Jesus says, "Don't be afraid.

Peace be with you."

"Jesus, is it really you?" says one friend.

Another friend says, "Maybe it isn't really Jesus. Maybe it's a ghost!"

A ghost! Some of the friends are afraid.

Jesus says, "Don't be afraid. Touch me and feel that I am real." *(Invite children to touch each others' hands.)*

Then Jesus says, "Do you have anything to eat? I'm hungry." They give him some fish to eat. *(Pass around the plate of food for the children to share.)*

The friends can touch Jesus. The friends can share food with Jesus.

"Jesus, it's really you!" the friends shout. "You're really alive!"

If you wish, discuss with the children:
■ How do Jesus' friends feel when they see Jesus?
■ Why does Jesus encourage his friends to touch him?
■ How would you touch Jesus if you could touch him? Would you give him a hug? hold his hand? sit on his lap?

Prayer

Encourage children to join you in calling out *Alleluia!* several times. Then invite them to respond with *Alleluia!* in this final prayer:
■ Thank you, God, for giving Jesus new life. *Alleluia!*
■ Thank you, Jesus, for being with us and for asking us to touch. *Alleluia!*
■ Thank you, God, for so many things... *(Encourage children to offer their own thanksgivings. Help children respond to each prayer by calling out* Alleluia!*)*
■ Thank you, God for each child here. *(Name each child, helping children respond with* Alleluia! *after each name.)*

Thank the children for joining you and invite them to return to their seats.